PENGUIN PLAYS

FOUR PLAYS

THE PRIVATE EAR
THE PUBLIC EYE
WHITE LIARS
BLACK COMEDY

One of the foremost dramatists of our time, Peter Shaffer was born in Liverpool and educated at St Paul's School and Trinity College, Cambridge. He had several varied jobs before earning fame as a playwright – working as a 'Bevin Boy' in the coal mines during the Second World War, in the acquisitions department of the New York Public Library and for the London music-publishing firm of Boosey & Hawkes.

His first big success came in 1958 with *Five Finger Exercise*. The play ran for nearly two years at the Comedy Theatre in London, and was subsequently presented, with great acclaim, in New York City. Other Shaffer successes include *The Private Ear: The Public Eye* (which, like *Lettice and Lovage*, starred Maggie Smith and played at the Globe Theatre); *The Royal Hunt of the Sun*, an epic drama concerning the Spanish conquest of the Inca Empire; the hilarious farce, *Black Comedy*; *The Battle of Shrivings*; *Equus*, a sensational triumph in London and in New York where it received the 1975 Tony Award for Best Play of the year; and *Amadeus*, which also won the same prize, as well as the 1979 *Evening Standard* Drama Award, the Plays and Players Award, and the London Theatre Critics' Award. Both these last mentioned plays boast the rare distinction of having run for over a thousand performances on Broadway and in 1984 the film of *Amadeus* won the Academy Award for both script and picture. His most recent plays are *Yonadah* and *Lettice and Lovage*. Penguin publish a number of his plays.

Peter Shaffer was awarded the CBE in the 1987 Birthday Honours List.

FOUR PLAYS

THE PRIVATE EAR
THE PUBLIC EYE
WHITE LIARS
BLACK COMEDY

PETER SHAFFER

PENGUIN BOOKS

PENGUIN BOOKS

Published by the Penguin Group
27 Wrights Lane, London W8 5TZ, England
Viking Penguin Inc., 40 West 23rd Street, New York, New York 10010, USA
Penguin Books Australia Ltd, Ringwood, Victoria, Australia
Penguin Books Canada Ltd, 2801 John Street, Markham, Ontario, Canada L3R 1B4
Penguin Books (NZ) Ltd, 182–190 Wairau Road, Auckland 10, New Zealand

Penguin Books Ltd, Registered Offices: Harmondsworth, Middlesex, England

The Private Ear and *The Public Eye* first published in Great Britain by
Hamish Hamilton 1962
Copyright © Peter Shaffer, 1962, 1964
White Liars and *Black Comedy* first published in Great Britain by
Hamish Hamilton 1968
Copyright © Reath Enterprises, 1967

This collection first published in Penguin Books 1981
3 5 7 9 10 8 6 4

Typeset, printed and bound in Great Britain by
Hazell Watson & Viney Limited
Member of BPCC Limited
Aylesbury, Bucks, England
Set in Monotype Bembo

CONTENTS

THE PRIVATE EAR

A PLAY IN ONE ACT

FOR
PETER WOOD
WITH LOVE

CHARACTERS

The Private Ear was first presented with *The Public Eye* at the Globe Theatre, London W1, on 10 May 1962, by H. M. Tennent Ltd. It was directed by Peter Wood; decor was by Richard Negri and lighting by Joe Davis. The cast was as follows:

TED	Douglas Livingstone
BOB	Terry Scully
DOREEN	Maggie Smith

THE PRIVATE EAR

The curtain rises on BOB's *bed-sitter in Belsize Park, about seven of a summer's evening. It is a shabby room on the top floor, with a window at the back looking out over a grimy London roof-scape. Besides the bed, over which hangs a large print of Botticelli's 'Birth of Venus', there is a frayed armchair, a chest of drawers, a table laid for three, and around it two chairs and a stool piled with cushions. The room is untidy, littered with papers and music magazines, and most noticeably it is dominated by the twin speakers of a stereophonic gramophone, attached to the sloping roof on either side of the window. The machine itself is downstage to the left (audience view), and attached to the nearby wall are shelves of records. Over to the right is the kitchen; through its sliding door can be seen a sink, a small refrigerator, and behind, another window opening on to the same flushed sky. The main door to the landing and stairs is downstage, beyond the kitchen.*

[*The room is empty. From outside the door we hear jazz, and* TED *strolls in carrying a transistor radio and a bunch of sweet peas. He is about twenty-five, cocky and extroverted, fitted out gaily by Shaftesbury Avenue to match his own inner confidence, and wearing a snappy hat and sun-glasses. His whole relationship to* BOB *shows an air of patronizing domination.*]

TED: Bob! Bob!
BOB [*off*]: Hello!
TED: I've arrived – and to prove it, I'm here! Where are you?
BOB [*off*]: In the bathroom. What time is it?
TED: Ten past seven. What time is she coming?

[BOB *rushes in, wearing a frayed dressing-gown and towelling his hair.*]

BOB [*a Lancashire accent*]: Half past.

[*He removes the towel to reveal an awkward young man in his early twenties, whose whole manner exudes a painful lack of confidence. During the ensuing scene with* TED *he dresses and makes himself presentable.*]

TED: Well, that's twenty minutes. You've got plenty of time. Just take it all nice and easy. I've bought you some flowers. Provides that chic touch to the decor you're a tiny bit in need of.

BOB: Pretty.

TED: You know, you ought to be flattered I'm here tonight, playing chef for you. Do you know where I could have been?

BOB: Where?

TED [*produces photo*]: With her. How about them for a pair of bubbles?

[BOB *takes photo.*]

And that hair. It's what they call raven black. It's got tints of blue in it. Lustrous, as the ad says. You can't keep your hands off it. See the way she holds herself? That's what they used to call carriage, my boy. Carriage. You don't see any carriage nowadays. Just fiddle and wiggle, that's all. Course, most of the girls you meet think they've got it – poor little nits. Toddling about on stilettos making holes in the lino. Carriage! Look at her. Miss Carriage!

BOB: Where did you meet her?

TED: At the Mecca last night, dancing herself giddy with some gorilla. I sort of detached her. She wanted a date for tonight, but I said – 'Sorry, girl, no can do tomorrow! I'm engaged for one night only as chef to my mate Tchaik, who is entertaining a bird of his own. Very special occasion.' So you be grateful. Greater love hath no man than to pass up a bird like this for his mate.

BOB: What's her name?

TED: You won't believe it if I tell you. Lavinia. Honest. Lavinia. How's that for class? The rest of it's not so good. Beamish. Lavinia Beamish.

BOB: She's beautiful.

TED: Do you think so?

BOB: I do – yes.

TED: She's going to go off fairly quickish though. In three years she'll be all lumpy like old porridge.

BOB: I don't know how you do it. I don't, really!

TED: Just don't promise them anything, that's all. Make no promises, they can't hang anything on you, can they?

BOB: I wouldn't know . . . I really am, by the way.

TED: What?

BOB: Grateful.

TED: Oh, forget it. It's only a bird, isn't it? Here, I heard a good one yesterday. The Tate Gallery just paid ten thousand pounds for a picture of a woman with five breasts. D'you know what it's called?

BOB: What?

TED: 'Sanctity'.

BOB [*not understanding*]: Sanctity?

TED: Un, deux, trois, quatre, cinque, titty . . . Come on, let's get on with this din, then. Half past, you say?

BOB: Quarter of an hour. That's if she comes at all.

TED: Of course she'll come. Why shouldn't she? It's a free dinner, isn't it?

[TED *has crossed to the laid table, and is now staring at it.*]

Well, for God's sake! Is that what you call laying a table?

BOB [*rising anxiously*]: What's wrong with it?

TED: It'd be great for the chimpanzee's tea party. [*Pointing to the place settings.*] This one's got three knives, and this one's got three spoons. Well done.

BOB [*hurrying to re-arrange them*]: Oh Lord! [*He upsets vase.*]

TED: You're in a state, aren't you? Tchaik's in a state! Pit-a-pat, isn't it? Pit-a-flippin'-pat!

BOB: Don't be daft.

[*Re-laying the table, he upsets the water jug.*]

TED: You've wet my Lavinia! . . . Well get a cloth! . . .

[BOB *runs to get a cloth.*]

13

[*To the photo*] We'll have to dry you out, love.

[*He places the photo on the mirror above the chest of drawers.* BOB *mops the table.*]

Look, what's up? It's just a girl, isn't it?

BOB: Yes.

TED: Well then. What's so special?

BOB: Nothing.

TED: All right. So she looks like a Greek goddess.

BOB: Look, Ted, I didn't say that. I just said her neck reminded me …

TED: All right, her neck. [*Picking up the bottle of wine*] What's this?

BOB [*pronouncing it like the flower*]: It's called Rose. The man in the Victoria said it'd go well with the lamb chops.

TED: Well, *he* didn't know what he was talking about, did he? Ignorant nit.

BOB [*alarmed*]: What d'you mean?

TED: Look and learn, will you? This is a *Rosé*. It's a light French wine. You drink it by itself, not with heavy meat like lamb. Get it? For that you want a claret or a burgundy. That's a Bordeaux or a Bourgogne. In any case you've got to serve this cold, can't you read? 'Servir légèrement frappé.' See? [*Pityingly*] He's quite hopeless. I'll put it in the fridge.

BOB: Is it going to be rotten, then?

TED: Well, it depends on your *taste*, doesn't it? Some people are happy with bottled cider. [*Seeing his face*] Oh, don't worry. *She* won't know the difference anyway. What do we start with?

BOB: Soup. I got two tins of mushroom. It's quite good if you add milk.

TED: In a Works canteen sort of way, I suppose. And what to follow?

BOB: Chops. Lamb. Do you have to unfreeze them first?

TED: They won't taste much either way. Not out of those bins in the delly. They never do. You should always go to a proper butcher, mate. [*Inspecting them*] A bit on the shaved side, aren't they?

BOB: They were the biggest they had.

TED: Well, just so long as I have that one! . . . Let's hope *she's* got a genteel appetite. Probably will have. Most girls think it's not really posh to eat a lot. [*Picks up a tin.*] These go with them?

BOB: Yes. Lamb and peas.

TED: You should have got petty pois, not these marrow-fats. It's more chic. You know – the little ones. The other size are sort of com.

BOB: They're not, are they?

TED: Definitely. Com. C.O.M. *She* won't know, mind you, but it's just the difference between class and no class, that's all.

BOB [*upset*]: Well, I'd better open them.

TED; That's my job, isn't it?

BOB: I can do it! [*He picks up the opener and starts cutting away furiously at a tin.*]

TED: Now look, don't get rattled: that's the worst thing you can do. Not with that pit-a-pat going . . . It's probably a good thing anyway not to have too much fancy scoff. That way she'll take pity on you, think you're not eating right and all that palaver. Needs a wife's good cooking. You know . . .

[BOB *cuts his finger on the tin and cries out.*]

BOB: Now look what I've bloody done!

TED: Steady on. You really are in a state, aren't you? Put it under the tap for a moment.

BOB: There's a plaster in that drawer!

TED [*going to chest of drawers and taking out a plaster*]: Well, pull yourself together for God's sake. You go on this way, the whole evening's going to be a flipping fiasco. You're not going to get far with any girl shaking blood over her cardigan. They're cowards that way. They can't stand the sight of blood on their woollies!

[BOB *comes in.*]

BOB: It's all right – just a nick.

TED [*dressing it*]: Give here. Now look, why don't you take yourself a snort and just sit down. I can cope in there. A gin and french, that's what you need.

BOB: There isn't any gin.

TED: I might have known. What are you going to give her first, then?

BOB: First?

TED: To drink.

BOB: Look, I didn't say she was a boozer, did I?

TED: You don't have to be a boozer to want a cocktail. It's the chic thing. No, it's not even chic. You can't ask her to sit down to eat just like that. [*Returning his finger*] You're really hopeless, aren't you?

BOB [*quietly, but with more firmness*]: I asked you to help, you know. Not to make comments.

TED: Well, help's one thing. This is just bricks out of straw, isn't it? Anyway, I didn't know I'd have to organize the whole *bit*! What's come over you? I know you've always been a bit on the twitch, but I've never seen you like this, all to pieces . . . What's she done to you? It's like the snake and the old guinea pig, isn't it?

BOB: Don't be daft.

   [*He moves away from him.*]

TED: Are you really serious, Tchaik?

BOB [*avoiding his eye*]: About what?

TED: This girl.

BOB: How can I be serious about someone I met for a few minutes?

TED: Well, I never know with you. You're deep. It's all that Celtic Twilight in your blood. That's not original, by the way. Miss Story said it in the office last week.

BOB: Who's Miss Story?

TED: You know – the old bag in accounts. She said you were mystic.

BOB: Yes, I'm sure.

TED: Seriously, is there anything?

BOB: I told you, don't be daft. Why should there be?

TED: Well, it's not every day you invite a girl to dinner, is it? Let's be honest. You go to hundreds of concerts, but you don't usually pick up a girl and invite her home for chops and vino, do you? So what gives?

BOB: I told you. We were next to each other.

TED: Yes?

BOB: I'd been watching her for ages out of the corner of my eye. She was absolutely beautiful. I couldn't believe it when she dropped her programme.

TED: Well, that was a piece of luck for you, wasn't it? Of course you handed it back with a mannerly bow?

BOB: I didn't, as a matter of fact. I didn't like to – in case she thought anything. It just lay there between us for about ten minutes. And then it was the interval, and I had to make up my mind. She was just going out when I picked it up and gave it her.

TED: And then what happened?

BOB: She said 'thank you'.

TED: That was original. Go on.

BOB: Well, I asked her if she liked music, and she said yes. It was a daft question, really, I suppose. I mean, she wouldn't have been there otherwise, would she? In the end it turned out she was on her own, and I asked her if she'd have a coffee with me after. I could hardly believe my ears when she said yes.

TED: Why not? Even goddesses get thirsty. So?

BOB: So we went to an espresso in South Ken.

TED: And held hands over two flat whites?

BOB: Not exactly, no. At a matter of fact, I couldn't think of very much to say to her. We were out in the street again inside of ten minutes.

TED: So that's why you asked me tonight? To help out with the talk?

BOB: I suppose, yes.

TED: I really am flattered. Your first date with her and you invite me along too.

BOB: Well, you know what to say to women. You've had the practice, haven't you?

TED: There's no practice needed. You just say the first thing that comes into your head: as long as it's not dirt, of course. They don't much like dirt, though they'll go for that too if you present it with a nice clean smile!

BOB: If I tried anything like that, I'd look like a seducer in a silent film.

TED: Well, you'd have to find your own style, of course. The important thing is, you've taken the plunge. You've invited a girl home!

BOB: Oh, I had to, in this case. There's no question about that. She was –

TED: What?

BOB: You'll laugh.

TED: No, I won't. Go on.

BOB: Well, the first girl I ever saw I wanted to see again. I mean, had to. She's got a look about her – not how people are, but how they ought to be.

TED: Steady on.

BOB: No, I mean it. When I said her neck reminded me, you know what I was thinking of?

TED: Who?

BOB [*indicating the Botticelli print*]: Her.

TED: Venus?

BOB: Yes. She's got exactly the same neck – long and gentle. That's a sign.

TED: A sign?

BOB: Yes.

TED: What for?

BOB: Spiritual beauty. Like Venus. That's what this picture really represents. The birth of beauty in the human soul. My Botticelli book says so. [*Snatching up a Fontana pocket library edition*] Listen. 'Venus, that is to say Humanity, is a nymph of excellent comeliness, born of heaven. Her soul and mind are Love and Charity. Her eyes, dignity. Her hands, liberality. Her feet, modesty.' All signs, you see. 'Venus is the Mother of Grace, of Beauty, and of Faith.'

TED: And your bird's the mother of all that?

BOB: No, of course not. I'm not a fool. But that look of hers is ideal beauty, Ted. It means she's got grace inside her. Really beautiful people are beautiful inside. Don't you see?

TED: You mean like after Andrews Liver Salts?

BOB: That's exactly what I mean.

TED: Oh, Tchaik, now seriously, come off it. I think that's daft. I mean it is, boy. There's a lot of stupid, greedy little nitty girls about who are as pretty as pictures.

BOB: I don't mean pretty.

TED: Then what?

BOB: Well, what you called carriage, for instance. What your Lavinia's got. It's not just something you learn, the way to walk and that. It's something inside you. I mean real carriage, the way you see some girls walk, sort of pulling the air round them like clothes. You can't practise that. You've got first to love the world. Then it comes out.

TED: I see. Have you got any red-currant jelly? They always serve it with lamb in chic restaurants.

BOB: I've got some jam.

TED: What kind?

BOB: Gooseberry.

[*The doorbell rings.*]

BOB: There she is!

TED: So I hear. Calm down. All right, now listen. The last swallow of coffee and I'm away. Deadline 9.30. Work to do at home. Got it? 9.30 you see me, 9.31 you don't!

BOB: Look, it's not like that at all.

TED: No? Well, if it isn't it *ought* to be . . . Go on, then!

BOB: Yes. The soup's in a tin.

TED: You showed me.

BOB: Good.

[*The bell rings again.* BOB *frantically puts on his coat and tries scooping up papers and hiding magazines under chairs.* TED *watches him coolly.*]

TED: Why not just leave her standing there? She'll go away in five
minutes.

[BOB *moves nervously to the door.*]

TED: Here!

[*The boy has left the cleaning slip on the sleeve of his coat.* TED *rips
it off. The pink tag inside the collar is more difficult to remove.* TED
has to bite it off. BOB *wriggles impatiently. The bell goes again.*]

BOB: Hurry up!

TED: Go on, then.

BOB [*hesitating*]: I wish I had a drink to offer her.

TED: Well, you haven't, have you?

BOB *goes out. Left alone,* TED *carefully combs his hair in front of the
mirror, shines his shoes on his trousers' legs and goes into the kitchen,
shutting the door.* BOB *returns with* DOREEN, *a pretty girl of about
twenty, wearing an imitation ocelot coat. It is at once obvious that she
is nervous also, and has no real pleasure in being there. Her reactions
are anxious and tight, and these, of course, do nothing to reassure the
boy.*]

DOREEN: I'm not too early?

BOB: No. Just right. [BOB *shuts the door.*]

BOB: Actually, it's only just half past. You're very punctual.

DOREEN: Unpunctuality's the thief of time, as my dad says.

BOB: To coin a phrase.

DOREEN: Pardon?

BOB: Let me take your coat.

DOREEN: Thank you. [*She slips it off. Under it she is wearing a jumper
and skirt.*]

BOB [*taking the coat*]: That's pretty.

DOREEN: D'you like it?

BOB: I do, yes. Is it real? I mean real leopard.

DOREEN: It's ocelot.

BOB [*hanging it up*]: Oh! [*Imitating* TED] Very chic.

DOREEN: Pardon?

BOB: Won't you sit down?

[*They advance into the room.*]

DOREEN: Is this all yours? Or do you share?

BOB: No, I live alone. There's actually a friend here at the moment. He's helping with the dinner. We work in the same office.

DOREEN: Can I help?

BOB: No, it's all done. Really. All you can do is sit down and relax. [*With an attempt at 'style' he gestures at the armchair.*]

DOREEN: Thanks. [DOREEN *sits in it. A tiny pause.*]

DOREEN: Well . . .

BOB: Do you smoke?

DOREEN: I do a bit, yes.

BOB: Good! Tipped or plain? [*He picks up a cigarette box and opens it with a flourish.*]

DOREEN: Well! That's luxury for you, isn't it – both kinds! Tipped, thank you.

BOB: Allow me. [*He picks up a lighter with his other hand and tries to snap it alight. It doesn't work. He puts down the box and fumbles with it, to no avail.*]

DOREEN: It's all right. I've got a match. [*Fetching matches from her handbag, and proffering the light.*]

[*He sits. Another tiny pause.*]

BOB: So, how have you been?

DOREEN: Fine. You?

BOB: Yes. Can't complain. Er . . . you're a typist, aren't you?

DOREEN: Stenographer. The place that trained me said 'Never call yourself a typist: it's lowering.'

BOB: Oh. What kind of things do you – well, stenog. I suppose?

DOREEN: The usual letters.

BOB: Yours of the tenth?

DOREEN: Pardon?

BOB: 'Dear Sir, in reply to yours of the tenth.' Things like that?

DOREEN: Oh, I see. Yes, that's right.

BOB: Do you mind it?

DOREEN: What?

BOB: Doing the same thing, day in, day out.

DOREEN: Well, there's not much choice, is there?

BOB: I suppose not.

DOREEN: You've got to earn your living, haven't you? Like my dad says, 'it doesn't grow on trees'.

BOB: No. Wouldn't they look odd if it did?

DOREEN: Pardon?

BOB: The trees.

DOREEN: Oh, yes. [*She looks at him nervously.*]

BOB [*plunging on*]: Like when people say unpunctuality's the thief of time – like your dad says. I always used to try and imagine unpunctuality in a mask – you know – with a sack labelled 'swag'. That's what comes of having a literal mind. I remember I had awful trouble at school one day with that poem which says 'The child is father of the man'. I simply couldn't see it. I mean, how could a child be a father? I couldn't get beyond that. I don't think imagination's a thing you can cultivate though, do you? I mean, you're either born with it or you're not.

DOREEN: Oh, yes, you're born with it.

BOB: Or you're not.

DOREEN: Yes.

BOB: There ought to be a sign so parents can tell. There probably is, if we knew how to read it. I mean, all babies are born with blue eyes, but no one ever says there's a difference in the blue. And I bet there is. I bet if you looked really hard at six babies the first day they were born you'd see six different kinds of blue. Milky blue – sharp blue, you know, like cornflower colour – even petrol blue. And they each mean something different about character. Of course, after the first day they all fade and become the same. It's a thought, anyway.

DOREEN: Oh yes!

BOB: Daft one. [*Desperately*] Would you like a drink?

DOREEN: Well, I wouldn't say no.

BOB: Good. [*Unhappily*] What would you like?

DOREEN: Whatever you suggest. I'm not fussy.

BOB: Gin and french?

DOREEN: That'd be lovely.

[*A brief pause. Then he rises quickly.*]

BOB: Well, if you'll just excuse me.

DOREEN: What are you doing?

BOB: I won't be a moment.

DOREEN: Can I help?

BOB: I won't be a second.

DOREEN: Where are you going?

BOB: Just round the corner. To the pub. It's only a step away.

DOREEN: Haven't you got any in?

BOB: No. I – [*inventing it*] – I don't drink.

DOREEN: You don't?

BOB: No.

DOREEN: Well, don't go on my account.

BOB: That's all right. I mean, I want to.

DOREEN: That's silly.

BOB: Why?

DOREEN: Because I don't drink either.

BOB: You're just saying that.

DOREEN: No, honest. I don't.

BOB: Ever?

DOREEN: Well, at Christmas and that. But I don't want one now. I only said it to be sociable.

BOB: You sure?

DOREEN: Positive.

BOB: Well, that's all right then.

DOREEN: Of course.

[*Pause.*]

BOB: You know, I always thought an ocelot was a bird.

DOREEN: Did you?

BOB: Yes. I must have been thinking of an ostrich.

[*Enter* TED *with two glasses of wine on tray, playing the waiter.*]

23

TED: Cocktails, madame? A little chilled vino before din?

DOREEN [*delighted*]: Ohh!

BOB: This is my friend, the one I told you about. Ted Veasey – Miss Marchant.

TED: Pleased to meet you.

DOREEN: How d'you do?

TED: Head above water and still swimming, thank you! You know, most people never answer that question – how do you do? That's because those who ask it don't really want to know. How do *you* do?

DOREEN: Oh, very nicely, thank you.

TED: That's all right then. Do I have to call you Miss?

DOREEN: Well, it is a bit formal, isn't it? Why don't you call me Doreen?

TED: Thanks. I will. If it's not too presumptuous. You see, I'm only the butler around here! [*Offers her a drink*] Madame?

DOREEN [*hesitating to take one*]: Well . . .

BOB: I'm afraid she doesn't drink.

TED: No?

DOREEN: Well, on special occasions.

TED: Well tonight's an occasion, isn't it? Of course, it is. A real proper [*French accent*] 'occasion'! Come on. Do you good.

DOREEN: Well . . . Just to be sociable.

TED: That's it. [*Offering drink to* BOB] Tchaik?

BOB: Well, you know *I* don't.

TED: Don't what?

BOB: Drink.

TED: Since when?

BOB [*unhappily*]: Well, always . . .

TED: First I've heard of it. You were sloshed last week.

BOB: I mean not before dinner.

TED: What?

BOB: Not on an empty stomach. You know I don't.

TED: Well, waste not, want not, I say! [*Drinks.*] Oh, the servants you get these days! . . . See you, my dear, in two shakes of a lamb's tail – or should I say, chop? [*He goes back into the kitchen.*]

DOREEN: He's funny.

BOB: Yes, he is. He's marvellous to have in the office. I mean, he's always cheerful.

DOREEN: Aren't you?

BOB: Not always, no.

DOREEN: What office do you work for?

BOB: Import–export. I'm just a glorified clerk, really. At least that's what Ted keeps on telling me, and I suppose he's right.

DOREEN: Why, is he over you?

BOB: In a way he is, yes.

DOREEN: What way?

BOB: Well, he's just been promoted to look after a small department of his own. It means quite a bit of responsibility. He's going to go a long way, I think. I mean he's interested and keen – you know.

DOREEN: But aren't you?

BOB: Well, not so much as he is. He knows all about economics. Tariffs and the Common Market. I'm afraid it's all rather beyond me.

DOREEN: I like people who want to get on. Who've got drive. That's something I respect. My dad's got drive. That's one thing he has got.

BOB: What does he do?

DOREEN: Well, he's retired now. He used to be a Works Manager.

BOB: Where?

DOREEN: Edmonton.

BOB: Oh.

DOREEN: He says, if you haven't got drive, you might as well be dead.

BOB: He's probably right. Is that drink all right?

DOREEN: Yes, it's lovely.

BOB: Good.

DOREEN: Cheerio.

BOB: Cheerio. [*Enviously, he watches her drink.*]

DOREEN: This is a nice room.

BOB: D'you like it?

DOREEN: Yes, I like large rooms.

BOB: So do I.

DOREEN: Most of the rooms you see today, they're tiny ... Like matchboxes.

BOB: Yes! [*He laughs obligingly, then rushes on eagerly.*] Mind you, that would suit some people. I saw a man in the Tube yesterday who looked exactly like a safety match. Thin body like a stick, and a tiny black head. I remember thinking: 'Bryant and May' could use you.

DOREEN: Pardon?

BOB: Bryant and May could use ...

[*He falls silent.* DOREEN *stares at him unencouragingly.*]

[*Plunging on*] Mind you, it's not that large, really. Not when you have to eat and sleep all in the one. Still, it's hard finding places, and they're very tolerant here.

DOREEN: Tolerant?

BOB: I mean, they don't interfere with your private weaknesses – you know.

DOREEN: Pardon?

BOB: I mean your habits. I'm afraid I've got rather a weakness, and some people would get a bit shirty about it, but not here. They let me play Behemoth all night, even past the music hours. [*Indicating the stereophonic machine*] That's him, of course. Behemoth means a great monster, you know. It's in the Bible.

DOREEN: What is it then, a gramophone?

BOB: Stereo.

DOREEN: It looks lovely.

BOB [*a new note of warmth and pride in his voice*]: You should hear him. Do you know anything about these animals?

DOREEN: I'm afraid not, no.

BOB: Well, I shan't bother you with technical names then. But I can tell you this is really the best machine a chap of my means could possibly afford, anywhere in the world. Of course, if you want to spend thousands, it'd be different. [*With an uncontrollable burst of true enthusiasm, the boy is off on his hobby-horse.*] Behemoth's a real marvel, I can tell you. Most big sets you can't play properly below a certain level. You can't hear them properly, unless they blast you out of your seat. That's because they've got bad speakers. [*Indicating*] These things. Most speakers have only got between five and seven per cent efficiency. These have got between fifteen to twenty. Wharfedale speakers. They're the best! ... I'm sorry: I promised not to give you technical names. It's the music that counts, anyway, isn't it? [*With great warmth*] I'm glad you like music. I can't tell you how glad I am to know that. You know, last week I'd been watching you for ages before you dropped that programme. I was watching you all through the Bach: and you were so wrapped up in listening, so concentrating, there were wrinkles all over your face!

[*She looks at him, startled and displeased. He falters.*]

Well, I mean, they were very becoming ... I love to see lines on people's faces. I mean, that's their life, isn't it? It's what's happened to them. Most girls you see have got so much powder and muck on, you can't tell anything's happened to them. You know, they're like eggs, their skins. Eggshells, I mean ... you're different.

DOREEN: You mean I've got inner beauty.

BOB: Do I?

DOREEN: That's what a man told me once. Inner beauty. It was his way of saying he was off me.

BOB: That's not what I mean at all. [*Desperately*] You know the really wonderful thing about this machine? You can turn it up as loud as you like and all you hear is the faintest hum. [*He switches it on.*] Listen, I'm going to turn it right up. [*He turns the volume control as far as it will go.*] See?

DOREEN [*blankly*]: Wonderful.

BOB [*happily*]: You must have been listening to music for an awfully long time to like Bach. Most people come to him only after a bit. When I first started it was all the Symphonie Pathétique and Swan Lake. You know.

27

DOREEN [*who has heard of this*]: Oh – yes!

BOB: That's why Ted calls me 'Tchaik': it's short for Tchaikovsky. I was mad about his music once. I thought Bach was boring, like exercises. Then one day I was shaving – isn't it daft how things happen? – I always play records when I'm shaving, or in the bath – and I'd put on one of the Brandenburgs, you know, the Fourth with two flutes, and suddenly – just suddenly – I heard what made it marvellous. It wasn't about love or victory, or those romantic things that change all the time. It was about things that *don't* change. D'you see what I mean?

[*She gives him a quick, tight smile, but says nothing.*]

Anyway, would you like to hear one? I've got all six.

DOREEN: Lovely . . .

BOB: Good. Well, if you wouldn't mind moving here, you'd enjoy it better. You'd be midway between the two speakers at just the right distance. Let me help you.

[*She gets up and he pushes her chair into the proper position.*]

That's it. [*He motions her to sit.*] Now . . . behold! [*He throws open a cupboard which is crammed full of records.*]

DOREEN [*impressed*]: Help! Are all those yours?

BOB: Every one!

DOREEN: But you must spend all your pay on records!

BOB: Well, you've got to spend it on something, haven't you? Which Brandenburg would you like? Or maybe you'd prefer the Goldbergs? or the Musical Offering?

DOREEN [*who has never heard of any of these*]: You choose.

BOB: No, it's your pleasure, madame!

DOREEN: Well, to be frank, I don't know that much about it. That old stuff isn't really me.

BOB: You mean you prefer Modern?

DOREEN [*seeing a gleam of hope*]: That's right. Modern.

BOB: What d'you like? Stravinsky? Shostakovich?

DOREEN: Well, I don't quite mean that.

BOB: You mean something more tuneful?

DOREEN: Yes.

BOB: Britten! Like me. I think Britten's the greatest composer in the world, I mean, he writes tunes, and makes wonderful sounds you can understand, not just plink-plonk. I hate all that twelve-tone stuff, don't you? It's sort of not – human. I know what I'll play you! [*Grabbing an album*] *Peter Grimes*! Decca's done the most marvellous recording of it ever. D'you know it?

DOREEN: I can't say I do.

BOB: It's the greatest thing you ever heard! It's all about this lonely fisherman who lives by himself, and the village hates him because he's different, and has dreams and visions about what life should be. He dreams about this girl, Ellen – someone to share his life, you know, only he's not very good at expressing himself. In the end the village turns against him and accuses him of killing his apprentice. There's a sort of manhunt at night – people calling and shouting, hurrying in with lanterns, makes up a posse – you know: it's terrifying. It's like a rising sea, getting wilder and wilder, up and up and up till it suddenly bursts over the town! [*Taking the record out of its sleeve and putting in on the turntable*] I think it's the most marvellous thing I ever heard. Listen!

> *He puts on the record at the moment in Act 3 of* Peter Grimes *when the lynch chorus begins its dangerous song of hate –* 'Him who despises us we'll destroy!' BOB *listens to it, entranced, beating time to its hurtling rhythms and mouthing the words, which he clearly knows.* DOREEN *watches him with something much less like involvement: she obviously detests the music.* BOB *has put it on very loudly: it becomes quite deafening as it boils up into the great shouts of* 'Peter Grimes!' *punctuated by silence.*]

[*Explaining in a hushed voice*] That's his name, 'Peter Grimes'. They all just stand there and call it. Sssh! . . .

> [*The chorus yells* 'Grimes!' *Silence.*]

[*Sings*] 'Peter Grimes!'

> [TED *comes in from the kitchen carrying a tray of soup: on his head is a chef's hat made from a grocery bag.*]

29

TED [*facetiously*]: Did someone call me?

[DOREEN *laughs.*]

[*Going over to the table and distributing the soup*] Turn it down for God's sake, or you'll have the neighbours in. Come on, dinner up. [*To* DOREEN] Madame!

DOREEN [*rising*]: Ooh, lovely.

[BOB, *his face set, stops the gramophone.*]

TED: Potage à la Heinz! Champignon! Note that 'g-n' sound, that's pronouncing it proper. Followed by lamb chops à la Ted Veasey.

[DOREEN *laughs delightedly and sits herself at the table.* TED *shakes out a napkin and spreads it over her lap.* BOB *is very elaborately switching off the set, and putting the record back in its sleeve. His movements are slow and mechanical.*]

DOREEN: Thanks very much.

TED: Hey, Tchaik, stop fussing with that damn thing, and come and be host. It's your party, isn't it? Now take a nice slice of Hovis, my dear, it goes beautiful with the soup! And have a fill-up on the rosé. Drinka pinta wine a day! . . . Here's to you! And you, chum!

[BOB *approaches the table, and sits down.*]

BOB [*responding quietly to the toast*]: Thank you. [*Firmly he pours out a large drink for himself.*] To you.

TED: You know, how you stand that stuff I'll never know. Opera! How so-called intelligent people can listen to it I just can't imagine. I mean, who ever heard of people singing what they've got to say? [*Singing to the tune of the Toreador Song in Carmen*] 'Will you kindly pass the bread?' 'Have a bowl of soup?' – 'Champignon!' – 'I must go and turn the gas off . . .' Well, for heaven's sake! If that's not a bloody silly way to go on, excuse language, I don't know what is. I wish someone would explain it to me, honest. I mean, I'm probably just dead ignorant.

BOB [*speaking very quietly*]: You are.

[TED *looks at him in surprise.* BOB *has never said anything like this before.* BOB *looks at him with calm contempt.*]

Dead ignorant.

[*A brief pause.* DOREEN *looks anxiously from one to the other.*]

TED: Come on. Drink up before it gets cold.

[*All three lift their spoons. They freeze. Dim out: spot only on* BOB.]

[*The next pieces of dialogue are* ON TAPE.]

DOREEN: Ooh lovely! Soup! Nice flavour.

TED: Well, let's say it shows willing, anyway. Warms you up on a cold night. like some others I could mention. Go on – dip your Hovis in it, that's the best way.

[DOREEN *laughs.*]

[*The tape speeds up to a mad chatter.* BOB *drinks off an entire glass of wine, quickly. The tape winds down to normal speed.*]

DOREEN: Ooh, lovely! Chops!

TED: D'you like 'em?

DOREEN: They're my favourite, actually – chops – they always were, ever since I was small. ! always used to like the way there was a meaty bit in the middle of the fatty bit.

TED: Yes. I know what you mean!

[DOREEN *giggles.*]

[*The tape speeds again, while* BOB *gulps still more wine, and then slackens once more to normal speed.*]

DOREEN: Ooh, lovely! Peaches!

TED: Yellow cling.

DOREEN: What's that?

TED: Their name.

DOREEN: It isn't!

TED: It is. Yellow cling peaches. Say, what a name for your Chinese girl friend. Yellow Cling Peach.

[DOREEN *laughs hilariously.*]

What time is it, then? What time is it, then? [*Louder, with echo*] *What time is it, then?!*

[END OF TAPE.]

BOB: Nine o'clock.

[*Lights up. They lower their spoons and resume the scene. It is now an hour later. The day has almost gone.* BOB *sits perfectly still, half in a world of his own.*]

TED [*to* DOREEN]: Some more vino, then?

DOREEN: I don't mind if I do.

TED [*picking up the bottle*]: Well, what d'you know? There isn't any. Tchaik's taken it all!

DOREEN [*giggling*]: I thought he didn't drink.

TED [*posh*]: Not on an empty stomach! [*To* BOB] You certainly make up for it on a full one.

DOREEN: Like my dad. Only that's cos he's got an ulcer. He can drink with his meal, but not before. If he drinks before, it's murder. He's chewed the carpet before now. Once he tore a lump right out of the fringe. Honest.

BOB: Poor chap.

DOREEN: Yes. He suffers terribly with it. Well, of course he's a worrier. A natural worrier. He worries about everything.

TED: Does he worry about you?

DOREEN [*a little stiffly*]: He's got nothing to worry about in that department.

TED: No?

DOREEN: No. I mean politics. Things like that. The way the world's going. I think his ulcer started to grow the day he was appointed to be Branch Secretary of the Union.

TED: Well, that's enough to worry anybody. He's a Union man, then?

DOREEN [*proud*]: All his life.

TED: Well, good luck to him

DOREEN [*indignant*]: What d'you mean?

TED: I'm a Tory myself and I don't care who knows it. Bloody unions. If you ask me, they're doing their best to ruin the country.

DOREEN: That's just stupid!

BOB: Yes. I agree.

TED: You can shut up for a start. You didn't even vote at the last election! Wherever you look you come back to the same thing. The Unions. Always at the bottom of everything, the Unions, demanding, demanding all the time. No settling day. Give them one thing, they want another, and another, and another till we're all bust – which we pretty nearly are now. The Unions! They make me bloody sick!

DOREEN: Well, I don't agree with you.

TED: And what do you know about economics? About the real laws that govern industry? Nothing. What do you care? Damn all! Well?

DOREEN [*cowed*]: Well – I don't know.

TED: 'Course you don't know.

DOREEN: Well, all the same! . . .

TED: What?

DOREEN: My dad can remember the time when he had to fight to get twopence halfpenny a week.

TED: Your dad.

DOREEN: Yes, my dad!

TED: And how old a gentleman would he be, may one ask?

DOREEN: Well, he's getting on now.

TED: How old?

DOREEN: Sixty-one.

TED: Well, there are you then. That's all in the past, isn't it? Of course the Unions were OK then: that was the bad old days. But it's become a cause now: the Union right or wrong. Eh, it's all so old-fashioned, the bosses against the workers! I can tell you one thing: if the Unions are going to run this country, I'm moving out. Because the rate they're going, they're going to bankrupt it completely and utterly inside ten years. Get the coffee, Tchaik. I'm worn out! Come on, give a hand, luv. [*Singing to the same tune*] 'That really was-a very lovely meal – Pass me the mats.'

DOREEN [*also singing*]: 'The knives and forks and spoons!'
    [*They both giggle.* BOB *looks on unsmiling.*]

TED [*singing*]: 'Where is the tray? – pom, pom, pom – Leave the flowers!' You've gone very quiet. Are you all right?

BOB: I'm fine.

TED: It's all that wine. [*To* DOREEN] Did you know alcohol is what they call a depressant?

DOREEN: No.

TED: That's something most people don't know. Most people think it's a stimulant, but they're wrong. Not in the long run it isn't . . .

[BOB *goes into the kitchen with the tray.*]

DOREEN: You know a lot, don't you? I like people who know things.

TED: Well, there's no good being an ignoramus, is there? You know things, you get on. Why don't you make yourself comfortable?

DOREEN: Thanks.

[*She rises and moves to the armchair.* TED *rises too, and deftly shuts the door so that* BOB *won't hear.*]

That was a smashing dinner.

TED: Glad Madame liked it.

DOREEN: I did, very much. You are clever.

TED: Oh ce ne fay rien! How d'you like Tchaik?

DOREEN [*without enthusiasm*]: He's nice.

TED: Certainly is, and a very good son to his old mother, which is more than you are, I bet. I mean daughter.

DOREEN: My mother's dead, smarty. And for your information, I look after my dad, which I bet is more than you do.

TED: Me? I look after Number One.

DOREEN: Yes: I bet!

TED: Well, the way I see it, I'm enough to look after. I haven't got time to take on anyone else. Anyway, Tchaik's lucky: his old lady's in Warrington. Anyone can be a good son to someone living in Warrington. You go down there, have a couple of days, high tea, eggs and chips, quick kiss and you're away! Now me, my people live practically on the doorstep. Hounslow. Well, that's different, isn't it? You're flipping right it is. 'Why can't you live at home?'

they say. 'You can have your own room.' My own room! I should just like to see me using my room for - well, for what I use a room. Am I being crude?

DOREEN: I think you are, yes.

TED: Tch, tch. Dear me! You'll have to take me as you find me, then, won't you?

DOREEN: I'm not sure I find you very nice.

TED: No?

DOREEN: No.

TED: Well, that depends on what you're looking for, doesn't it?

DOREEN: Pardon?

TED: I find you smashing. I do, honest. I bet there's a lot of fun in you, once you loosen up.

[She looks at him startled.]

Oh, I don't mean that way. I don't know what you think of me.

DOREEN: Do you care?

TED: 'Course I do.

DOREEN: Well, if you're like most boys, your mind's on just one thing.

TED: Well, I'm not like most boys. I'm me! And my mind's on lots of things. What's *your* mind on, most of the time? That's when you're not looking after Dad or going to Prom Concerts? What's with that, anyway? I don't get it. You're not the concerty type.

DOREEN: You're Mr Know-all, aren't you?

TED: Well, are you?

DOREEN: No, as a matter of fact, I was given a ticket by a girl friend. She couldn't go, and it seemed silly to waste it. Now he thinks I'm a music lover, and know about Bach and everything. Actually it was ever so boring.

[TED laughs loudly.]

Ssh! . . . I realized I shouldn't have said 'Yes' to him for tonight as soon as he asked me.

TED: What made you?

DOREEN: Well, I don't know. I don't get out that much. And he was very nice. Very courteous.

TED: I bet.

DOREEN: A blooming sight more better mannered than what you are.

TED: Well, who's denying it? Tchaik's always had manners. He's one of Nature's gentlemen.

DOREEN: You're wicked, you know. You really are.

TED: I mean it. He's a good boy. He wouldn't hurt a fly – and that's not because he's a fly himself either. Because he isn't. He's got feelings inside him I wouldn't know anything about – and you neither.

DOREEN: Thanks.

TED: I mean it. Real deep feelings. They're no use to him, of course. They're in his way. If you ask me, you're better off without all that dreamy bit.

DOREEN: What d'you mean?

TED: Dreams. Visions.

DOREEN: You mean he *sees* things?

TED: 'Course not.

DOREEN: What then?

TED: Well, he has ideas about perfect women. He's got one about you.

DOREEN: He hasn't.

TED: He has. Why d'you think you're here? How many girls do you think he's ever asked here?

DOREEN: I dunno.

TED: None. [*Spelling it*] N-o-n-e.

DOREEN: Well, what's he want with me then?

TED: Nothing. You're a vision. You've got a long neck like Venus coming out of the sea.

DOREEN: Who's she?

TED: He thinks you're the dead spit of *her*. [*He takes down the print from the wall and shows it to her.*]

36

DOREEN: Oh, I haven't got a long neck like that!

TED: I know you haven't. Yours is the standard size, but he won't leave it at that. He's got to *stretch* it a bit. A long neck's a sign of a generous nature!

DOREEN: He's a bit nutty, isn't he?

TED: Not really.

DOREEN: I think he is. When he was talking about that record his eyes went all glary.

TED: Oh, that's nothing. Just the old Celtic Twilight in him.

DOREEN: Twilight?

TED: Just a phrase. [*He rehangs the picture.*]

DOREEN: You don't half have a way of putting things. You've got a gift for words, haven't you?

TED: Always had. Words, languages. It's why I took up French in the evenings.

DOREEN [*admiringly*]: I like that.

TED: Do you? Most people would say it was pretentious. Then most people make me sick! They've got no drive, no ambition, nothing. I reckon now we're going into the Common Market we all ought to learn French. I bet you typists will have to speak it before long.

DOREEN [*alarmed at this thought*]: You don't mean it?

TED [*amused at her alarm*]: Of course. Why not?

DOREEN: Are you serious?

TED: 'Course I am [*Cruelly*] You'll be out of a job, then, won't you? [*A brief pause. He smiles thinly.*]

DOREEN: You're pulling my leg.

TED [*producing transistor*]: I wouldn't mind trying.

DOREEN: Oh! Isn't it smashing.

TED: Do you dance?

DOREEN: I like to, yes.

TED: I bet you're really something on the floor.

DOREEN: Pardon?

TED [*fake American accent*]: I bet you swing, Doreen, baby, I bet you're a real kooky kid!

[*He starts to dance, shaking his pelvis at her. Noiselessly,* BOB *slides open the kitchen door and starts to carry in the tray of coffee. What he hears stops him.*]

TED [*over*]: You ever been to the Mecca?

DOREEN: No.

TED: You'd like that. It's really nice. Classy, you know. None of that cave-man stuff. Of course, if you do a bit of a wriggle, no one exactly minds.

[*She laughs.*]

I'll take you there if you like.

DOREEN: When?

TED: Any time. You name it.

DOREEN: Well, I'm not sure I'd like it.

TED: 'Course you would. It's good clean fun, as they say. Honest – none of that touch-you-up and look the other way! Straight up. What about next Friday? They have a Late Night Special Fridays, eight to one.

DOREEN: No, next Friday I'm busy.

TED [*not to be put off*]: Friday after then? [*Stopping*] Well?

DOREEN [*suddenly capitulating*]: All right.

[BOB *closes the door again.*]

TED: Good. You'd better give me your phone number, then.

DOREEN: No, I'll meet you there.

TED: I can't have you going there on your own. I'll have to pick you up. That's if you don't live in Norwood, or some lousy place like that.

DOREEN: No. Putney.

TED: You're lucky. That's just inside my cruising area! [*Serious*] You're all right, you know. You've got it.

DOREEN: Got what?

TED: Oh, that certain something. It used to be called carriage. People nowadays call it class, but it's not quite the same thing.

[BOB *comes in with his tray of coffee cups and pot.*]

[*Seeing him: with false breeziness*] Well – I'm away? I'll just have my coffee, and allez. Love you and leave you!

DOREEN [*disappointed*]: Oh! Why?

TED: Duty calls. [*Executive voice*] All that work I took home from the office, clamouring for my attention!

DOREEN: Go on!

TED: Well, that's my story, and I'm stuck with it. [*To* BOB] No sugar.

BOB: Sorry. [*Goes into kitchen.*]

TED: Ciggy?

DOREEN: No, thank you.

TED [*offering her the pack*]: Go on.

DOREEN: No, really.

TED [*Sotto voce*]: Telephone.

DOREEN: What?

TED [*through clenched teeth*]: Number.

DOREEN [*understanding*]: Oh. Well, give me a pencil, then. I –

[BOB *returns.*]

[*Flustered*] It's lovely coffee. It tastes really continental. Like it's been perking for hours in one of those machines. Italian . . . [*She becomes aware of the cigarette packet in her hand, and that* TED *is holding a pencil.*] Can I have the little girl's room?

BOB: It's out on the landing. I'll show you.

[*She rises, crosses to the chest of drawers for her handbag and deftly takes the pencil from* TED.]

DOREEN: It's all right. I can find it.

[*She goes out, giving* BOB *a quick smile. There is a pause. The two boys look at each other.* TED *is the first to break the silence with a nervous laugh.*]

TED: Well, it's nine thirty. I'm off. Count ten and I'll be gone. I wish I was in your shoes. I do honest. Not going home to my empty bed-sit. I tell you, mate, your card is definitely marked. We're frying tonight! What's the matter?

BOB: Nothing.

TED: Are you all right?

BOB: That's like 'How d'you do', isn't it? There's no answer expected. [*He goes into the kitchen.*]

TED: What? ... Now pull yourself together, Tchaik. Don't start that pit-a-pat going again. What have you got to worry about? I've chatted her, and she told me she likes you a lot. She thinks you're the most courteous man she ever met. That's her actual word for you – *courteous*. If you ask me, it's time you stopped being so flipping courteous. Get off your knees. This is a girl, that's all. Not a goddess. And no girl wants to be worshipped, whatever she may tell you. You just give her a shove off her pedestal, you'll find she won't exactly resent it.

[BOB *comes out of the kitchen, his face set.*]

BOB: Go home, Ted.

TED: I am going home. The only reason I'm still here at 9.32 belting back my coffee, it because you seem in dire danger of jeopardizing your immediate succulent prospects. And that upsets me. It makes me feel I've wasted my time. After all, I've gone to no little trouble to ensure the success of this enterprise.

BOB: What?

TED: Well, haven't I? What do you think I've been doing here all evening?

BOB: I don't know. You tell me.

TED: What's the matter with you? You've been hitting the vino a bit, haven't you? You asked me here tonight to set it up for you. And that's what I've done. Just that. I've knocked myself out for you this past two hours, breaking her in nice and easy. Flowers on the table – chilled wine before dinner – the old sexy dance after-wards to get her in the proper receptive mood. To say nothing of cooking the bloody meal itself. And all for you.

BOB: For me?

TED: Of course for you. Who else? That's why you asked me here, isn't it? To give you the benefit of my savoir-faire – for what it's worth!

BOB [*suddenly exploding*]: Savoir-faire! D'you know something? You're so ignorant, it's pathetic!

TED: Ignorant? ... That's twice in one night. If I'm so ignorant I'd better take myself off.

BOB [*opening the door for him*]: Why don't you?

TED: *Ignorant!* That's lovely, that is. Well, I'll know better next time, won't I? I'll know better than to ever help anyone again!

BOB: You don't know what help is. You do your best as you see it, but what if that's *nothing*, what you see? You'll have lived in vain!

[TED *slams the door violently.*]

TED: Don't you lecture me, boy! It's not me who doesn't help. It's you, you who doesn't want it. Maybe that's your whole bit, Tchaik. You *want* it all to be a bloody total disaster. Christ knows why . . . Well, you've got your wish.

BOB [*turning to him*]: That's all very clever, Ted, but it doesn't mean anything at all. D'you think I'm half-witted?

TED: I told you what I think.

BOB [*violently*]: Yes, I know! I'm someone to look down on, aren't I? Teach tricks to! Like a bloody monkey. You're the organ grinder, and I'm the monkey! And that's the way you want people. Me, or her, or anyone! . . . Well – go home, Ted. Find yourself another monkey!

[DOREEN *returns. A long pause.* BOB *has his back to* TED *and won't turn round.* TED *tried to say something – to patch it up – make a joke – anything – but nothing comes. He gives it up and with a sudden rough gesture walks past* DOREEN *and slams out of the room.*]

DOREEN: Where's he going?

BOB: Home.

DOREEN: Home?

BOB: Yes.

DOREEN: You mean he's not coming back?

BOB: I don't think so, no.

DOREEN [*unable to take it in*]: You mean he's just gone off like that without even saying goodnight?

BOB: Well, yes . . . He had work to do at home, very urgent. Remember, he did say.

DOREEN: Did he?

BOB: Yes. And he won't let anything stand in the way of his work. [*Bitterly*] That's what's called drive.

DOREEN: Have you two had words, then?

BOB: No.

DOREEN: What about?

BOB: Nothing.

DOREEN: Was it about me?

BOB: Of course not! Why should it be?

DOREEN: I don't know I'm sure. [*She goes to the door, opens it, and disappears onto the landing.*]

BOB: Here – drink your coffee. It's getting cold.

DOREEN [*returning*]: I think that's the rudest thing I ever heard of. Ever, in my whole life.

BOB: He didn't mean it that way.

DOREEN: Well, what way did he mean it then?

BOB: Oh hell, I don't know. Drink your coffee.

DOREEN: I don't want it.

BOB: Then leave it!... I'm sorry.

DOREEN: Don't mention it.

BOB: It's my fault really.

DOREEN: Why?

BOB: I've had too much to drink. I can't carry it. Alcohol's not really a stimulant at all, you know. It's a depressant.

DOREEN: I know. I heard.

BOB [*smiling*]: He means well, you know. He really does. You can't hold things against him.

DOREEN [*hostile*]: Why not?

BOB: Because that's the way he is. He's like that in the office – off-hand, always joking ...

DOREEN: Yes. I bet he'll have a joke about *me* tomorrow.

BOB: Of course not.

DOREEN: I bet ... What office would that be, anyway?

BOB: I told you. Import–export.

DOREEN: No, I mean the actual address.

BOB: The address? What for?

DOREEN: Nothing. I just asked. [*She slips the pencil and cigarette packet into her bag.*] It must be nice having someone in the office you're close to.

BOB: We're not close.

DOREEN: I though you were friends.

BOB [*passionately*]: Well, we're obviously not! ... Why should we be? We only work in the same office – we've nothing in common ... No one in the office is close. That's what's wrong with them. You don't get to know anyone except in a special small way. An awful petty roll-on-five-thirty sort of way! ... But you're different. You know people at once, without having to try.

DOREEN: I don't know about that.

BOB: Oh, it's true. It's the obvious thing about you. Now what would you say about me at first sight? That I was a clerk? Would you?

DOREEN: Not specially, no.

BOB: Then what? Because I don't know. I don't know who I am. I suppose that's the point of education. Finding out who you really are. I never had that.

DOREEN: Why not?

BOB: Well, when I could have done, I didn't want it. I hated school.

DOREEN: So did I.

BOB: I hated it so much I took the first job that came along.

DOREEN: What did you come down here for?

BOB: When Dad died I came south. If I could start again, I'd *make* myself study.

DOREEN: Well you could if you wanted. You're still young. You could go to night-school.

BOB: No.

DOREEN: Why not? Your friend does.

BOB: Well, of course, he's got *drive*. You lot go on about drive, but you can't have drive without enjoying your work. Now Ted does. When he leaves the office he's as fresh as a daisy, but when I come home I've hardly got the energy to grill a chop, let alone pick up a French book, – and what have I done? Filled in about

sixty invoices. What a way to spend your day, with all the possi-
bilities in you. And some of those people have been doing it for
thirty years. Taking endless dictation. Typing thousands of meaningless letters. 10th of the inst. 11th ultimo. C.I.F. E. & O.E.
Thanking you in anticipation. Your esteemed order. Are you going
to spend the rest of your life being someone else's obedient servant,
top copy and two carbons?

DOREEN: Well, like I say, we haven't got much choice, have we?

BOB: Yes, we have. We must have. We weren't born to do this.
Eyes. Complicated things like eyes weren't made by God just to
see columns of twopence halfpennies written up in a ledger!
Tongues. Languages. Good grief, the woman next to me in the
office even *sounds* like a typewriter. A thin, chipped old typewriter, always clattering on about what Miss Story said in accounts
and what Mr Burnham said back. It's so *wrong*! ... Do you know
how many thousands of years it took to make anything so beautiful,
so feeling, as your hand? People say 'I know something like the
back of my hand,' but they don't know their hands. They wouldn't
recognize a photograph of them. Why? Because their hands are
anonymous. They're just tools for filling invoices, turning lathes
round. They cramp up from picking slag out of moving belts of
coal. If that's not blasphemy, what is? ... I'll tell you something
really daft. Some nights when I come back here I give Behemoth
a record for his supper. That's the way I look at him sometimes,
– feeding off discs, you know. And I conduct it! If it's a concerto I
play the solo part, running up and down the keyboard, doing the
expressive bits, everything. I imagine someone I love is sitting out
in the audience watching – you know – someone I want to admire
me ... Anyway, it sort of *frees* things inside me. At great moments
I feel shivery all over. It's marvellous to feel shivery like that. What
I want to know is, why can't I feel that in my work? Why can't
I – oh, I don't know – feel bigger? ... There's something in me I
know that's big. That can be excited, anyway. And that must
mean I can excite other people, if only I knew what way ... I
never met anyone to show me that way.

DOREEN: Well.

BOB: Well.

DOREEN: Well, I really must be going now.

BOB: You're quite pretty, you know.

DOREEN: Thanks.

BOB: I mean, very pretty really. Please stay, just a little longer.

DOREEN: I'm afraid I can't. My dad will be worrying about me.

[*She takes her coat from behind the door. He helps her into it.*]

BOB: Does he worry that much about you?

DOREEN: Yes, he's a natural worrier.

BOB [*urgently*]: Well, how about one more record before you go?

DOREEN: Worries about everything.

BOB: One for the road.

DOREEN: Old people always do, don't they?

BOB: Something more tuneful and luscious? I know – *Madam Butter-fly*! [*He rushes to his record collection.*] D'you know the Love Duet? You'll like that! I know it's awfully corny, but I do love all that fudgy sort of music. At least I have great sort of cravings for it. Like I suppose some people have for chocolates. [*Offering the record to her.*] Try a bit.

DOREEN: Well really, it is getting awfully late.

BOB [*with desperate appeal*]: It only takes three minutes.

[*She hesitates.*]

DOREEN: Well – all right.

BOB [*excited again, as he switches on the machine*]: You know what's happening, don't you? Pinkerton – that's the American sailor – has married this Japanese girl in spite of her family and the priests and everybody. And this is the first time they're alone together . . .

[*He puts on the record, not looking at her, at the start of the Love Duet from* Madam Butterfly, *beginning with the quiet orchestral music before* 'Vogliatemi bene, un bene piccolino'. *Butterfly begins to sing.*

There now ensues a Six-minute Sequence in which not a word is spoken. At first both stand – he by the gramophone, she by the door – in atti- tudes of strain. Then the warmth of the music gives BOB *the courage*

45

to gesture her towards the armchair, and she tiptoes across the room and sits in it.

She listens for a moment, and finds it surprisingly pleasant. She smiles. He sits on the stool near the table, then surreptitiously edges it nearer to her. He reaches out his hand to touch the ocelot coat; she notices this, and the boy hastily mimes a gesture to indicate smoking. She nods. He rises eagerly, and gets her the cigarettes: in his nervousness he opens the box of matches upside down, and they scatter all over the floor. They pick them up together. Finally, kneeling, he lights her cigarette – then, fascinated by her prettiness, he stares up at her. The flame of the match burns between them until she gently blows it out.

She offers him a puff: he declines – then accepts. He inhales and chokes a little. He takes her hand and begins to study it with intense concentration. The music increases in ardour.

Suddenly DOREEN *is sorry for him. She closes her eyes and lowers her face to be kissed. Lightly, hardly daring, he responds by kissing her forehead. She opens her eyes a little impatiently, and tugs at her ocelot coat: it is rather hot, isn't it? With clumsy fingers he helps her out of it, and she makes herself more comfortable, tucking her legs under her in the chair. Then again she closes her eyes and invites his kiss.*

This time he touches her lips. Clumsily, hardly knowing what to do, his arms grope for her body. The eagerness of his response surprises and alarms the girl. She begins to struggle as the boy's excitement grows. Their positions in the chair become increasingly ridiculous, as she seeks to avoid his embrace with her legs trapped under her. Above them the voices of the operatic lovers sing ecstatically of love. Finally, DOREEN *struggles free:* BOB *is left lying in an absurd position across the armchair.*

He stands up, rumpled and upset. He is no longer listening to the inhuman, undisturbable lovers: he is desperate. Slowly, his mind full of how TED *would act under these circumstances, he begins pursuing her: as slowly, she retreats to the corner of the room, and stumbles back on to the bed. The boy falls softly on top of her, and tries with a deep*

46

muddled gentleness to show her passion. She tries haplessly to avoid him. Finally she half rises and pushes him to the floor. Then she gets up, adjusts her clothes, and moves away from him across the room.

BOB *stares at her. Then he, too, gets up, and comes towards her with a gesture at once desperate and supplicating. Puccini's Love Duet rises to its climax. As the final, unifying chord of deliciousness crashes over the room,* DOREEN *slaps the boy's face – then, horrified, takes it between her hands, trying to recall the blow. Slowly* BOB *backs away from her across the width of the room. The music dies away; the record turns itself off. Silence hangs between them.* BOB *speaks at last.*]

BOB: I'm sorry. [*He switches off the gramophone.*]

DOREEN: That's all right.

BOB: No, no, it isn't. It isn't at all. [*Long pause*] Actually, you see, I've brought you here under false pretences. I should never have asked you. You see. I didn't really tell you everything about myself. That was wrong of me. Please forgive me.

DOREEN: What d'you mean?

BOB: Well, you see, actually I'm engaged.

DOREEN: Engaged?

BOB: Yes. To be married.

DOREEN [*really surprised*]: *You* are?

BOB [*defiantly*]: Yes. Yes. So I shouldn't have asked you here. I'm sorry. [*She stares at him. He is not looking at her. On a sudden impulse he picks up the photograph of the girl left by* TED.]

DOREEN: Is that her?

BOB: Yes.

DOREEN: Can I see?

[*He passes it to her.*]
She looks lovely.

BOB: Yes, she is, very. That's really raven black, her hair. It's got tints of blue in it. You can't really judge from a photo.

DOREEN: What's her name?

BOB: Er . . . Lavinia. It's rather an unusual name, isn't it? Lavinia. I think it's rather distinguished.

47

DOREEN: Yes, it is.

BOB: Like her. She's distinguished. She's got a way with her. Style, you know. It's what they used to call carriage.

[*She gives him a startled look.*]

So you see . . . well – no harm done, I suppose.

DOREEN [*dully*]: No, of course not.

BOB: Here's your coat.

[*He helps her with it. She is hardly listening to him.*]

I wonder why I thought an ocelot was a bird. I wasn't thinking of an ostrich. It was those pictures you see of ladies in Edwardian photos with long, traily feathers in their hats. Is there such a thing as an osprey?

DOREEN: I wouldn't know. [*With a smile*] It's not really ocelot, you know. It's lamb dyed. And it's not really cold enough for fur coats anyway, is it, yet? I was showing off.

BOB: I'm glad you did.

[*They go to the door.*]

DOREEN: Well, it's been lovely.

BOB: For me, too.

DOREEN: I enjoyed the music. Really.

BOB: Good.

DOREEN: Perhaps we'll meet again. At a concert or somewhere.

BOB: Yes. Perhaps we will.

DOREEN: I'm glad about your girl. She looks lovely.

BOB: She is.

[*They avoid each other's look.*]

DOREEN: Well, good night.

BOB: Good night. [*He opens the door and lets her out. Then he suddenly calls after her*] Fabian and Carter!

[*She reappears.*]

DOREEN: Pardon?

BOB: The name of the firm. Where Ted works. You wanted to know it. Fabian and Carter. Bishopsgate 2437. Good-bye.

[*She gives him a quick nod, and goes. He shuts the door. For a moment he doesn't move – merely stands with closed eyes. Then his gaze comes to rest on the gramophone. He moves towards it, his face hard and fixed. He looks down at it. Then once again he puts on the record of* Butterfly. *As it begins to play he kneels to the machine, stretching out his hands to enfold it. Then suddenly he draws his hands back. He takes off the pick-up and with a vicious gesture scratches the record beyond repair.*

A pause. The boy replaces the pick-up. Again the Love Duet is heard filling the room, but now there is a deep scratch clicking through the music, ruining it. The stage darkens. BOB *stands rigid beside* Behemoth.]

SLOW CURTAIN

THE PUBLIC EYE

A COMEDY IN ONE ACT

FOR
VICTOR
WITH LOVE

CHARACTERS

The Public Eye was first presented with *The Private Ear* at the Globe Theatre, London W1, on 10 May 1962, by H. M. Tennent Ltd, with the following cast:

JULIAN	Kenneth Williams
CHARLES	Richard Pearson
BELINDA	Maggie Smith

THE PUBLIC EYE

The curtain rises on the outer office of CHARLES SIDLEY, *Chartered Accountant, in Bloomsbury. It is a well-furnished room in white, gold and russet, with many white bookshelves laden with works of reference bound in leather. There is a desk where a secretary customarily sits, a sofa, and two doors. One leads out into the hall of the building, the other into* CHARLES' *office and is marked:* Private. *When the door is open we can see stairs going up to higher floors.*

It is mid-morning, and sunlight streams brightly through a large window.

[*On a chair sits* JULIAN CRISTOFOROU, *studying a large turnip watch. He is a man in his middle thirties; his whole air breathes a gentle eccentricity, a nervousness combined with an air of almost meek self-disapprobation, and a certain bright detachment. He is bundled in a white raincoat, with many pockets. Sighing, he drops the watch into a large leather bag, like a Gladstone, which is beside him. Then he reaches into one pocket and extracts a large handkerchief, which he spreads over his knees; from another he produces a packet of raisins and pours them out; from a third, a packet of nuts, and does likewise. He just begins to eat them when he cocks his ear, hastily stuffs the handkerchief away in a fourth pocket and sits upright and unconcerned as the inner door opens and* CHARLES SIDLEY *comes out.*

CHARLES *is a good-looking man of forty, exact and almost finicky in his speech, with a fairly steady line in pompous sarcasm, and another, more immediately concealed, in self-pity.*]

JULIAN: Good morning.

CHARLES [*surprised to see him*]: Good morning.

JULIAN: Mr Sidley?

CHARLES: Correct.

JULIAN: I'm delighted.

CHARLES: You want to see me?

JULIAN: It's rather more that I have to. Not that I don't want to see you, of course.

CHARLES: Well, I'm sorry, but I was just on my way home. The office isn't really open on Saturday mornings; I was just doing a little work.

JULIAN: I know. I saw you.

CHARLES: I beg your pardon?

JULIAN: I peeped into your office before. But you were so engrossed I didn't like to disturb you.

CHARLES: How long have you been waiting, then?

JULIAN: About half an hour.

CHARLES: Half –

JULIAN: Oh, please don't apologize. It's a positive joy to wait in a room like this. There are so many delights to detain one. Your reference books, for instance. Overwhelming!

CHARLES: Thank you.

JULIAN: I perceive you have a passion for accuracy.

CHARLES: Let's say a respect for fact.

JULIAN: Oh, let's indeed. I do admire that. And in an accountant a first essential, surely. Mind you, one must be careful. Facts can become an obsession. I hope they aren't with you.

CHARLES: I hope so, too. Now, if you don't mind – perhaps I can make an appointment for next week.

JULIAN [*ignoring him, staring at the shelves*]: Websters! Chambers! Whittakers Almanac! Even the names have a certain leathery beauty. And how imposing they look on shelves. Serried ranks of learning!

CHARLES [*brutally*]: Are you a salesman?

JULIAN: Forgive me. I was lapsing. Yes, I was once. But then I was everything once. I had twenty-three positions before I was thirty.

CHARLES: Did you really?

JULIAN: I know what you're thinking. A striking record of failure. But you're wrong. I never fail in jobs, they fail me.

CHARLES: Well, I really must be getting home now. I'm sorry to have kept you waiting, even inadvertently. May I make an appointment for you early next week?

JULIAN: Certainly. If that's what you want.

CHARLES: Well, as I say, I don't receive clients at the weekend. Now let me look at my secretary's book . . . What about next Tuesday?

JULIAN [*considering*]: I don't really like Tuesdays. They're an indeterminate sort of day.

CHARLES [*with a touch of exasperation*]: Well, you name it, Mr –

JULIAN: Cristoforou. [*He pronounces it with an accent on the third syllable.*]

CHARLES: Cristoforou?

JULIAN: Yes. It's a little downbeat, I admit. Balkan cigarettes and conspirator mustaches. I don't care for it, but it's not to be avoided. My father was a Rhodes Scholar. I mean he was a scholar from Rhodes.

CHARLES [*with desperate politeness*]: Oh yes?

JULIAN: Why don't you call me Julian? That's a good between-the-wars name. Cricket pads and a secret passion for E. M. Forster. That's my mother's influence. She had connections with Bloomsbury. To be precise, a boarding house.

CHARLES: Would you please tell me when you would like to see me?

JULIAN: It's rather more when *you* would like, isn't it?

CHARLES: I have no special relationship with the days of the week, Mr Cristoforou.

JULIAN: Oh no more have I, in the final analysis. I mean they don't actually prevent me from doing things on them. They merely encourage or discourage.

CHARLES: I suppose I could squeeze you in late on Monday if it's urgent.

JULIAN: I had imagined it was. In fact, I must admit to feeling disappointed.

CHARLES: I'm sorry –

JULIAN: No, if the truth be known, extremely surprised.

CHARLES: Surprised?

JULIAN: At your being so off-hand. I had imagined you differently.

CHARLES: Are you in some kind of trouble?

JULIAN: Your trouble is mine, sir. It's one of my mottoes. Not inappropriate, I think. Still, of course, I mustn't be unreasonable. It's your decision. After all, you're paying.

CHARLES: I'm what?

JULIAN: Paying. [He makes to go out.]

CHARLES: Mr Cristoforou, come here. I had assumed you were here to see me professionally.

JULIAN: Certainly.

CHARLES: Well?

JULIAN: Well, it's more you wishing to see me, isn't it? Or hear from me anyway.

CHARLES: Perhaps you'd better state your business with me very precisely.

JULIAN: You mean to say you don't know what it is?

CHARLES: How can I?

JULIAN: You don't know why I'm here?

CHARLES: I haven't the faintest idea.

JULIAN: How appalling. I'm agonized. I'm really *agonized*! What must you think of me? Chattering away and you not even knowing why I'm here. Well of course I'd assumed – but then you shouldn't assume anything. Certainly not in my business. I'm afraid it's absolutely typical of me. My wits are scattered when they should be most collected. You haven't got a spoon on you by any chance?

CHARLES: A spoon?

JULIAN: For my yoghurt. Forgive me, it's a distressing symptom of nervousness which I've never been able to conquer. I always eat when I'm embarrassed. Or, as in this case, agonized. [He takes out a carton of yoghurt from his pocket.]

CHARLES: Mr Cristoforou, I'm not noted for my patient disposition.

JULIAN: I'm glad to hear that. Patience too long controlled turns to cruelty. That's an old Persian proverb. At least I think it's Persian. It could be Hindu. Do you have a dictionary of proverbs?

CHARLES [*bluntly*]: Who are you?

JULIAN: I'm Parkinson's replacement.

CHARLES: Replacement?

JULIAN: From Mayhew and Figgis. Now there are two names which are quite inappropriate for a Detective Agency. They should be Snuffmakers to the Duke of Cumberland or something like that. Don't you agree?

CHARLES: Are you telling me that you are employed by Mayhew and Figgis as a private detective?

JULIAN [*producing a china canister labelled* Sugar, *and attempting to pour some on his yoghurt*]: Of course. What else? I'm here to make our monthly report. The office was to telephone you and say I'd be coming today. They obviously failed. Very embarrassing. For both of us. [*Referring to the canister.*] That's empty.

CHARLES: And you are here in place of Parkinson?

JULIAN: Exactly.

CHARLES: Why? Where is he?

JULIAN: He's not with us any more.

CHARLES: You mean he resigned?

JULIAN: No. He was thrown down a lift shaft in Goodge Street. Do you know it? It's just off the Tottenham Court Road.

CHARLES: I know where it is.

JULIAN: Hazards of the game, you know. No one mourns him more than I. [*He opens the desk drawer and extracts a spoon.*] Where there's a secretary, there's always a teaspoon.

[CHARLES *stares at his visitor in disbelief. Then impulsively he picks up the telephone.*]

What are you doing?

[*Grimly* CHARLES *dials.*]

CHARLES: Hello? Mayhew and Figgis? This is Mr Sidley. Mr Charles

Sidley. I'd like to speak to Mr Mayhew. If he's not there I should like his home number. Yes. Good. Thank you.

[*Unconcernedly* JULIAN *eats his carton of yoghurt and looks out of the window.*]

[*Irritably*] Hello? Mr Mayhew? Mr Sidley here. I have a man in my office at this moment calling himself Cristoforou. He claims to be an employee of yours. What? ... Yes? ... Oh, I see. Yes, he told me that. Goodge Street. Yes, *I know where it is!* Very regrettable. A most efficient man. [*Looking at* JULIAN, *surprised*] He is? Well I hope I can, Mr Mayhew. I hope I can. This is a very delicate matter, as you know. What? No, of course I understand that: yours is a firm of the very highest – Yes, I say I know: yours is a firm of the very highest – Yes, yes, of course: I realize that. Naturally. Yours is a firm of the very highest – [*Pause*] Well, we'll see, Mr Mayhew. I am always willing to give people the benefit of the doubt, though I may add that when I say doubt in this case, I mean doubt. Good morning. [*He hangs up.*] You have a garrulous employer.

JULIAN: Only where he feels his honour to be at stake. After all, his is a firm of the very highest.

[*He smiles his bright smile.* CHARLES *glares.*]

In this case he said I'd been with it for three years and did the most expert work. Yes?

CHARLES: Correct, as it happens.

JULIAN: Well, it happens to be true. At the risk of sounding forward, I am a superb detective. It's one of the few jobs where being non-descript is an advantage. [*He takes off his raincoat to reveal an astounding striped suit underneath.*]

CHARLES: One would hardly describe you as nondescript, Mr Cristoforou.

JULIAN: Oh yes. I attained nondescript a long time ago. Last year I became characterless. This year, superfluous. Next year I shall be invisible. It's rather like one of those American Gain Confidence Courses in reverse. Make Nothing of Yourself in Six Easy Lessons! ... Actually I've been working on your affair for four weeks.

Mayhew's is a large agency, and we often take over each other's assignments. It's quite routine.

CHARLES: All the same, a little high-handed, I'd say.

JULIAN: I'm sorry you'd say that.

CHARLES: In any case, how did you know I was here?

JULIAN: I am a detective, Mr Sidley. You work here every Saturday morning, and your wife goes to the Cordon Bleu for a cooking lesson.

CHARLES: Correct.

JULIAN: It was an obvious opportunity to come around.

CHARLES: I see. Very thorough I'm sure. Now perhaps you would oblige me by reading your report.

JULIAN: Of course. That's why I'm here.

CHARLES: One would never know it.

[JULIAN *sits down and gropes in the Gladstone bag. He struggles with it for a moment and produces not the report, but an immense plastic bag of macaroons.*]

JULIAN: Would you like a macaroon? Excuse me. It's really disgusting, this eating business, I know. I have a friend who's a lawyer, and he gets so nervous about speaking in court, he eats sweets all day long. In his last murder case he devoured twenty-six Mars Bars in a morning. You're not a lawyer, are you?

CHARLES: No.

JULIAN: Of course not; an accountant. Silly of me. Scattered wits again! That's almost like being a priest today, isn't it? I mean, people do what you tell them without question. [*He takes out his report.*] What did poor Parkinson tell you at your last meeting?

CHARLES: Surely you know that already, if you inherited his assignment.

JULIAN: His report was negative.

CHARLES: Correct.

JULIAN: Your suspicions were unfounded.

CHARLES: So he said. The point is, are they still? A month has gone by since then.

JULIAN: That rather depends on what they were, doesn't it?

CHARLES: You know very well what they were. What they always are when you call in a detective. Are you trying to be humorous?

JULIAN: I sometimes succeed in being humorous, Mr Sidley, but I never try. Suspicion is a highly subjective word. It refers with exactitude only to the man who entertains it.

CHARLES: Mr Cristoforou, what do I have to do to get from you the information I am paying for?

JULIAN [*reasonably*]: I don't know what that is, Mr Sidley. If you wish to know whether your wife is being sexually unfaithful to you, I must point out that it is extremely difficult for a private eye to witness copulation.

CHARLES: How dare you?

JULIAN: It's even more difficult to witness the *desire* for copulation. Inevitably, therefore, there is no proof that your wife has slept outside her marriage bed.

CHARLES: No proof.

JULIAN: None whatever.

CHARLES: Then you have nothing to tell me.

JULIAN: I wouldn't say that.

CHARLES: Then what would you say? In a word, what – would – you – say?

JULIAN: I haven't got a word.

CHARLES: *Then find one!*

JULIAN [*hastily*]: Perhaps I'd better read my report. [*The detective picks up his report and tries to open it. Unfortunately the pages seem to be gummed together.*] Oh dear. That's syrup.

CHARLES: What?

JULIAN: I tried to transport a waffle yesterday, but it didn't work.

[*He tries for a long moment to separate the pages of his report. It tears badly. He looks at his employer with hapless eyes.* CHARLES *stares back in a thunderous silence.*]

[*Ingratiatingly.*] Well, I can read the first page anyway. [JULIAN *picks up the first page, which is in two bits, and reads in an official voice.*] 'Report by J. Cristoforou on the movements of Mrs Charles Sidley.

'Wednesday: September 22nd.' That was my first day, you see.

CHARLES: Never mind about that.

JULIAN: '10.48: subject leaves house. Takes taxi at corner of Walton and Pont Streets.' That's always a tricky one, by the way. Have you ever considered what one does if one's quarry hails a taxi and there isn't another one in sight?

CHARLES: I'd always assumed you drove a car.

JULIAN: Ah, sadly no longer. I used to be the ace driver of the agency. But one day I found myself in my car – a lightning-fast Volkswagen, painted chameleon brown – when I spotted on the pavement a wanted criminal of immense notoriety. Pablo Ibanez – an Iberian burglar – known to the police of six outraged countries as The Spanish Fly! Suddenly he caught my eye focussed upon him – always an unnerving experience – and he began to run! I gave chase, still in my car. To evade me he darted through the door of a large church, and I had no choice but to follow.

CHARLES: In your car?

JULIAN: There wasn't a moment to lose!

CHARLES: What happened?

JULIAN: I crashed into the baptismal font and ruined a christening. The baby fainted. The man got clean away, and later sent a jeering letter to the agency from Andalusia. As a result they took away my driving licence.

CHARLES: Would you continue with your report? My wife was in a taxi.

JULIAN: Yes, and on this occasion – most luckily – I was able to hail another. [Reading] 'Subject proceeds to Madame Martha, hatmaker, of 32 Marble Street.'

CHARLES: Could you see in?

JULIAN: Yes.

CHARLES: Who was there?

JULIAN: Four old ladies.

CHARLES: Any men?

JULIAN: I don't think so.

CHARLES: You don't think?

JULIAN: I mean they may have been dressed as ladies. It's just a possibility in a hat shop.

CHARLES: I see.

JULIAN: 'Subject collects hat, which appears to be already ordered, and emerges, wearing it. Hat resembles a wilted lettuce. Very unbecoming.'

CHARLES: Watch what you say, please. Everything my wife knows about hats, or clothes of any kind, she learned from me. When I first met her she wore nothing but sweaters and trousers. When you criticize her taste in hats, you are criticizing me.

JULIAN: I'm terribly sorry.

CHARLES: I suppose it's only natural that now she's moved away from me she should revert to type. All this last week she's worn nothing but a hideous black sombrero.

JULIAN: You don't like it?

CHARLES: You do?

JULIAN: I think it has a certain gamin chic.

CHARLES: Continue, please.

JULIAN: '11.30 subject in *exquisite* green hat walks up Brompton Road, enters the Michelangelo Coffee Bar. Orders a Leaning Tower of Pisa.'

CHARLES: What the hell's that?

JULIAN: A phallic confection of tutti frutti, chocolate chips, nougat, stem ginger, toasted almonds and molasses – the whole cloud-capped with cream! . . . Your wife is rather partial to it. So, as a matter of irrelevant fact, am I. Do you have a sweet tooth?

CHARLES: Never mind about my teeth. What happened next?

JULIAN: '12.17 subject rises and goes into Kensington Gardens. Walks to the statue of Peter Pan.'

CHARLES: What did she do?

JULIAN: She looked at it and laughed. A curious reaction, I thought.

CHARLES: Not at all. The first week we were married I showed her that statue and explained to her precisely why it was ridiculous. When you criticize her taste in statuary you criticize me.

JULIAN: Please forgive me. I don't know where to look.

CHARLES: At your report.

JULIAN: Yes ... Certainly ...

CHARLES: She was waiting for someone, I presume.

JULIAN: On the contrary, she wandered about quite aimlessly.

CHARLES: How do you know it was aimlessly?

JULIAN: At one point she picked up some acorns.

CHARLES: Acorns?

JULIAN: Yes, to throw at the ducks; I got the impression she had nothing better to do.

CHARLES: Charming! That's the result of all my work, trying to teach her to spend her leisure properly.

JULIAN: It was a very nice day.

CHARLES: What's that got to do with it?

JULIAN: I was trying to be indulgent.

CHARLES: You're not paid for indulgence, are you?

JULIAN: No.

CHARLES: Then get on.

JULIAN: Yes. '12.55 subject leaves park and enters a cinema in Oxford Street. It was showing the film "I was A Teenage Necrophile".'

CHARLES: Did you go in after her?

JULIAN: Naturally.

CHARLES: And she sat by herself?

JULIAN: Throughout. Four hours and seventeen minutes.

CHARLES: Four hours ...?

JULIAN: She saw it twice.

CHARLES: What did you make of that?

JULIAN: I thought it argued the most amazing capacity to suspend disbelief.

CHARLES: Indeed.

JULIAN: It was a very tasteless film. But worse ones were to follow. I mean on subsequent days.

CHARLES: And that was how she spent her day?

JULIAN: Yes.

CHARLES: After all I've taught her. How dare she? . . . How dare she??! . . . [*Upset*] I beg your pardon. It's not an easy thing to set detectives on your wife. It must seem rather bad form to you – or it would if – well.

JULIAN: If I wasn't one myself. It still does, Mr Sidley. I must admit I end up despising many of our clients.

CHARLES: Despising? That's rather rich coming from you, isn't it?

JULIAN: Oh yes, I dare say. It's something of a reflex action. They despise me, after all.

CHARLES: What else do you expect?

JULIAN: Nothing. The client looks down on the whore who relieves him. It's a familiar pattern.

CHARLES: Charming image.

JULIAN: But not inappropriate, I think.

CHARLES: If you think like that, why do you do it?

JULIAN: Private reasons. Or, to be exact, public reasons.

CHARLES: I don't understand.

JULIAN: It's not important. At the risk of seeming impertinent, Mr Sidley, why did you come to us? You really had nothing to go on.

CHARLES: You mean nothing concrete. No letters written in a hot, impetuous hand. No guilty smiles or blushes. My dear man, we live in the twentieth century, which blushes at nothing. The blush has gone out, like the ball-card and the billet-doux. Betrayal has become a word with rather quaint connotations.

JULIAN: I think that's just rhetoric, Mr Sidley. Rather well managed, if I may say so, but not true at all.

CHARLES: No? My wife has no more conception of sexual fidelity than that chair. When I married her, she thought nothing of sleeping with three different men in the same week.

JULIAN: Was one of them you?

CHARLES: I don't think I need to answer that.

JULIAN: Oh come. If you're like a priest in your profession, I'm like a psychoanalyst in mine. You can't afford to withhold information.

Unlike an analyst, I'm not considered a gentleman, so you can tell me everything. If this was true, why did you marry her?

CHARLES: Because . . . I was infatuated with her.

[*A pause.* CHARLES *almost visibly unbends a little.*]

JULIAN: Continue, please.

CHARLES: I don't see what possible bearing this could have on the situation.

JULIAN: Oh! But you must let me be the judge of that. Where did you meet her?

CHARLES: In a place called the Up-to-Date Club in Soho.

JULIAN: It doesn't seem the sort of place you would go to.

CHARLES: I was taken there by a journalist friend. I must say it was very pleasant. It had a dining-room upstairs with French cooking and a sort of cellar below where you could dance. I wasn't very good at dancing - at least not all that jungle warfare they call dancing - but the food was delicious, and Belinda served it.

JULIAN: Belinda?

CHARLES: My wife. She didn't serve it very well either; she was always forgetting one's order and having to come back for it - which I found more agreeable than otherwise . . . I caught myself going there rather often. Finally I asked her out to a theatre. She'd never seen anything more complicated in her life than a horror film. She was absolutely obsessed by horror films.

JULIAN: She still is.

CHARLES: Yes . . . It was a curious courtship. Without my demanding it, of course, she surrendered her whole life to me, for remaking. In a way, I suppose it wasn't too surprising. She'd lived in Northampton for the first eighteen years: her father was in shoes - and his ambitions for her extended no further than a job at the library and marriage with a local boy. Very properly she ran away to London, where she led the most extraordinary life, sharing a flat with two artists, one of whom baked his canvases in an oven, whilst the other spat paint onto his direct from his mouth - thereby expressing contempt for society, I believe. It's not surprising really, since at the time she was comparing them both to El Greco, that she reacted to some tactful reform with enthusiasm. For my part, I taught her everything I could. I'm not an expert, Mr Cristoforou: I'm that old-fashioned, but I hope not too comical thing, a dilettante. Of course the notion of an accountant with what, in the days when Europe was the world, used to be called a soul, probably strikes you as ludicrous. I'm afraid there's a great deal about this situation which is ludicrous. The moral, of course, is that men of forty shouldn't marry girls of eighteen. It should be a prohibition of the church like consanguinity: only marry in your generation. And yet it began so well . . .

JULIAN: You were happy?

CHARLES: Deeply. She renewed my life. I had someone to share things with: show things to.

JULIAN: And she? Did she show things to you?

CHARLES: She didn't need to. She was young and that was enough. Youth needs only to show itself. It's like the sun in that respect. In company with many men of my age, I found I was slipping away into middle life: journeying, as it were, into a colder latitude. I didn't like it. I didn't like it at all.

JULIAN: So you went after the sun. Tried to bottle a ray or two.

CHARLES: Foolish, imbecile attempt. Within a year I had to recognize that I had married a child. Someone with no sense of her place at all.

JULIAN: Her place?

CHARLES: Certainly. Her place. Belinda is the wife of a professional man in a highly organized city in the twentieth century. That is her place. As I have often explained to her, this would undoubtedly be different if she were wedded to a pop musician, which she seems to think she is. There is no such thing as a perfectly independent person.

JULIAN: Is that what she wants to be?

CHARLES [irritably]: I don't know what she wants to be. She doesn't know herself. Things have got steadily worse. Three months ago

68

I invited a very important client to dinner, the President of one of the largest investment companies in the City. My wife presided over my table dressed in what I can only describe as a leather pajama suit. When I remonstrated with her, she said she was sick of stuffy guests.

JULIAN: It's a fair point.

CHARLES [*hotly*]: It's not a fair point! [*Exasperated*] My friends are not stuffy, Mr Cristoforou, just because they don't come to dinner disguised as motor cyclists. No doubt they are helplessly out of touch with modern living. They only read, think, travel, and exchange the fruits of doing so pleasurably with each other. Is there anything so utterly boring and ridiculous as the modern worship of youth?

JULIAN: Nothing, no. It's like sun worship. Debasing and superstitious.

CHARLES [*looking at him suspiciously*]: No doubt this is very amusing to you.

JULIAN: How can you think that?

CHARLES: You think it's sour grapes?

JULIAN: Of course not!

CHARLES: Oh yes!

JULIAN: Mr Sidley, I beg you –

CHARLES [*with real pain*]: Has my wife a lover?

JULIAN: What makes you think she has?

CHARLES [*in a defeated voice*]: Because for three months now she has turned away from me. Just turned away. You know how women avert their faces when they don't want to be kissed. Well, she is averting her face, her look, her mind. Everything. Whole meals go by in silence, and when she talks, she appears not to be listening to what she herself is saying. In the old days she used to stay in bed until long after I'd gone to the office. I used to remonstrate with her about it. Now she's up and out of the house sometimes before eight. As if she can't bear to lie in my bed another minute . . . Last week one morning she was up at six. When I asked her where she was going, she said she wanted to watch the sun come up on Parliament Hill. [*Explosively*] God damn it, d'you think I'm a fool? She's seeing someone else, isn't she? Look – last night she didn't come in at all!

JULIAN: At all?

CHARLES: Well, not until well past two. And not one word of explanation.

JULIAN: Did you ask her for one?

CHARLES: If I ask her for anything, that's a quarrel in a minute. [*Pause.*] Tell me. There's someone else, isn't there?

JULIAN [*quietly*]: Yes.

CHARLES: Go on.

JULIAN: I find this hard.

CHARLES: Go on. How often do they meet?

JULIAN: Every day.

CHARLES: Every day?

JULIAN: Yes.

CHARLES: Describe him.

JULIAN: Well . . . he's handsome, I'd say.

CHARLES [*bitterly*]: Of course.

JULIAN: Full of a kind of confidence: you know – debonair, well dressed. I'd say he was a diplomat.

CHARLES: A diplomat? . . . There was that party at the Nicaraguan Embassy.

JULIAN: No, he's definitely not Nicaraguan.

CHARLES: How do you know that?

JULIAN: Ah! That's a very fair point. You have an acute mind, Mr Sidley. I admit that when you meet a complete stranger for the first time there is no definite way of knowing he's not Nicaraguan.

CHARLES: How does he behave to her?

JULIAN: With great politeness. He shows a most striking restraint.

CHARLES: You mean they don't actually kiss in public?

JULIAN: Certainly not!

CHARLES: What *do* they do, then?

JULIAN: Oh ... stare at each other happily. Exchange looks of deep meaning. Give those little secret glances – you know – I think the French call them 'œillades'. I'm sure that's the word. Shall I look it up?

CHARLES: Secret glances ...

JULIAN: I'd say, watching from a distance, their relationship was one of the utmost tenderness.

CHARLES: Would you?

JULIAN: Yes, I would.

CHARLES: Damn her!

JULIAN: Mr Sidley –

CHARLES: Damn her! Damn her!! [*Furiously*] What's his name?

JULIAN: I don't know.

CHARLES: Where does he live?

JULIAN: I don't know.

CHARLES: Liar!

JULIAN: I don't.

CHARLES [*grabbing him*]: Listen to me. You're a private detective, aren't you?

JULIAN: You know I am.

CHARLES: And it's your job to find out names and addresses?

JULIAN: I suppose it is.

CHARLES [*shaking him*]: Well you find out this man's name and address by tonight, or I'll break your bloody neck! [*He hurls him down on to the sofa.*]

JULIAN: Mr Sidley! You've no right to handle me like this. I'm a professional man.

CHARLES: You're a sneaking, prying, impertinent little wog!

JULIAN: I didn't want to tell you. You made me. Be honest. You made me.

[*A buzzer sounds. Pause.* CHARLES *goes to the inter-com on the desk and speaks.*]

CHARLES: Yes? Who is it?

BELINDA [*through the inter-com*]: Surprise, surprise!

CHARLES [*to* JULIAN, *amazed*]: My wife! She hasn't been here in over a year. You'll have to slip out the back way. [*Indicating the inner office.*]

JULIAN: Why?

CHARLES: Do as I say.

JULIAN: No.

[*The buzzer sounds again.*]

BELINDA: Charles?

CHARLES: I'm coming. Through there, down the fire escape, into the mews!

JULIAN: No.

CHARLES: Please. I'm sorry I pushed you. You're quite right, you're a professional man. I apologize. Only please go!

JULIAN: No.

CHARLES: Why not?

JULIAN: I haven't finished my report. There's lots more yet if I can unglue the pages.

CHARLES: Look, come back on Tuesday.

JULIAN: I told you I hate Tuesdays.

CHARLES: Well, Monday then. Six o'clock.

JULIAN: Five o'clock.

CHARLES: Five-thirty.

JULIAN: Done!

[*He stares at* CHARLES *and then goes into the inner office, shutting the door. The buzzer goes again.* CHARLES *answers it.*]

CHARLES: Yes.

BELINDA [*off*]: What's going on up there?

CHARLES: Nothing, my dear.

BELINDA [*off*]: Well, open the door then. It's still locked.

CHARLES: Oh! Yes – I'm sorry.

[JULIAN *comes quickly back into the room.*]

What is it *now*?

JULIAN: My macaroons!

72

CHARLES: Oh, for God's sake!

JULIAN: I can't possibly go without them. They're flown in daily from Vienna!

[*He rushes out again just as* BELINDA *appears screened by an enormous armful of yellow flowers. She lowers them to reveal a pretty young girl of twenty-two, wearing a coloured blouse, slacks and a black sombrero.*]

CHARLES [*coldly*]: Why aren't you at the Cordon Bleu?

BELINDA: I got tired of learning the right way to hold a saucepan, so I left.

CHARLES: And came here.

BELINDA: Obviously.

CHARLES: Why?

BELINDA: I was just passing.

CHARLES: Passing?

BELINDA: Yes. I thought I'd collect you. Surprise, lovely surprise. [*Seeing the carton left by mistake on the desk*] Who eats yoghurt?

CHARLES: I do.

BELINDA: Since when? I thought you loathed it.

CHARLES [*picking it up*]: Did you? Aha! Well you don't know everything about me.

BELINDA: I'll buy some for home.

CHARLES [*tasting it*]: No thank you.

BELINDA: Why not? If you like it.

CHARLES [*testily*]: I like it in the office. I do not like it at home. It's as simple as that.

BELINDA: Are you feeling all right?

CHARLES: Perfectly.

BELINDA: Well you don't look it. [*She dumps flowers into the vase.*]

CHARLES: Belinda, this is only my office.

BELINDA: I know where it is, Charles, and it needs them. Aren't they lovely? There was a man at the corner selling them off a barrow. I think he was a Malayan. At any rate he had topaz eyes, so I bought the lot. Two pounds ten with the greenery. The

Malayan said if I bought everything there'd be no monsoon over my temple for a year. Wasn't that a sweet thing to say?

CHARLES: Fairly uninspired, I should say. The gypsy who sold you one sprig of heather last week for five pounds did rather better.

BELINDA: That was because he belonged to a dying race, and I couldn't bear it. How awful it must be to belong to a dying race. Like the Yaghan Indians. I read somewhere there were only nine Yaghans left, right at the bottom of the world. No, honest! South Chile. After a while Nature says, 'Scrap them,' and they just fail, like crops. Isn't it sad? Imagine them. Nine little shrunk people, sitting on green water, waiting to die.

CHARLES [*grimly*]: I am imagining them.

BELINDA: What's the matter with you?

CHARLES: It's a pity I'm not a Yaghan Indian, isn't it? I might get a little attention from you. Yes. Outrageous demand for a husband to make of a wife, isn't it? Attention. Notice.

BELINDA: I notice you, Charles.

CHARLES: Very humorous.

BELINDA: It's not meant to be.

CHARLES: Where were you last night?

BELINDA: Out.

CHARLES: You knew I was bringing someone back.

BELINDA: You said you *might*.

CHARLES: Well, I phoned you from here at six and you weren't home.

BELINDA: Well, so? Did you need me to pour out whisky or cut his cigar?

CHARLES: That's hardly the point.

BELINDA: It's just the point, I'd say. You always say you want me to entertain your friends, and as soon as you can, you get out the port and send me out of the room. It's incredible, anyway, that a man of your age should be pushing decanters of port clockwise round a dining table. It makes you look a hundred. When I tell my friends, they can't believe it.

CHARLES: I'm sure they can't. But then one would hardly accept their notions of etiquette as final, would one?

BELINDA: Oh, please!

CHARLES: What?

BELINDA: Not your iceberg voice. I can't bear it. 'One would hardly say.' 'I scarcely think.' 'One might hazard, my dear.' All that morning-suit language. It's only hiding.

CHARLES: Indeed?

BELINDA: Yes, indeed. Indeed, indeed! People don't say 'indeed' any more, Charles. It's got dry rot.

CHARLES: Where were you?

BELINDA: With my friends.

CHARLES: Oh, of course. In some grotesque little coffee bar, I suppose.

BELINDA: Correct, as you would say.

CHARLES: Telling stories about me, The way I talk. The words I use. My behaviour at dinner. Very loyal, I must say.

BELINDA: And where were you? In a stuffy old Club, surrounded by a lot of coughing old men with weak bladders and filthy tempers, scared of women and all mauve with brandy. How lovely!

CHARLES: That's just disgusting.

BELINDA: You're telling me! ...

CHARLES: And where are you going now? I mean, where are you *passing* to go to? Another coffee bar?

BELINDA: Perhaps.

CHARLES: Belinda, what does Wife mean?

BELINDA: What?

CHARLES: Perhaps it's a word no one has ever explained to you. Certainly they didn't in that squalid little registry office you insisted on going to, because you couldn't enter a church. Nevertheless, at the risk of appearing still more pompous, my dear, you made a contract with me. A contract of marriage.

BELINDA: Well, what about it? There's nothing in it that says a woman must drop her friends and take her husband's. I know it's always done, but I don't see it should be. I never promised to cherish all those mauve old men in sickness and health. I love my friends: how can I be faithful to you if I'm unfaithful to them?

CHARLES: May I ask what that means?

BELINDA: That you're not my only duty, that's what it means, and I'm not yours. You've got to be faithful to all sorts of people. You can't give everything to just one. Just one can't use everything. And you certainly can't *get* everything from just one. Just because you get sex from a man, it doesn't mean you're going to get jokes as well, or a someone who likes jazz. Oh, I know a husband claims the right to be all these things to a woman, but he never is. The strain would be appalling.

CHARLES: Charming.

BELINDA: It's true.

CHARLES: It's not true! You talk about men as if they were hors d'œuvres: him for the herring, him for the mayonnaise, him for the pickled beetroot.

BELINDA: But that's exactly it! How clever of you to think of a comparison like that. That's marvellous!

CHARLES: Yes, well, it's just stupid and immature. I suppose I really shouldn't expect anything else.

BELINDA: Ta very much.

CHARLES: If you were a real woman, you wouldn't find it hard to receive everything from one man. To see everything in him and hope to be everything in return. But it's beyond you, of course.

BELINDA: Ta very much.

CHARLES: Oh stop that!

BELINDA: Then *you* stop it!

CHARLES: Listen to me, and try to understand. Stop fiddling with those flowers.

BELINDA: Well?

[*A slight pause.* CHARLES *collects himself.*]

CHARLES: Let me tell you something. Each man has all of these things inside him: sex, jokes, jazz and many other things than that.

He's got the whole of human history in him, only in capsule. But it takes someone who loves him to make those capsules grow. If they don't grow, he's not loved enough. And that kind of love can only be given by an adult.

BELINDA: Which I'm not. Thanks for nothing! Well, if I'm not, whose damn fault is it? This isn't my home. It's my school.

CHARLES: That's not true.

BELINDA: Oh but yes it is, Charles. Just look at the way you're holding that ruler! [*A pause. She looks at him seriously.*] You *were* everything to me once. I thought you were the most fantastic person I'd ever met. I remember the exact moment I fell in love with you. It was half past three on Thursday afternoon February the nineteenth two years ago. You had already explained to me the Theory of Natural Selection, the meaning of Id, Ego and Super-Ego, and were halfway through the structure of Bach's Fugue in C Sharp Minor, Book One, *Well-Tempered Clavier*. I thought to myself, 'How can one head hold so much? He's not showing off, these things come up naturally in his conversation.' I adored it. The world seemed so wide suddenly. You were the first person who showed me that an intellectual was a marvellous thing to be. Most of my friends are all feelings. They're just like moles bumping about in dark little burrows of feeling. And that was me too. Feeling, feeling all the time – but never getting to understand anything. When you met me, I'd have said or done anything just to join in. I thought people would like me more if I liked what they liked. So I pretended all the time. In the end I couldn't tell what I really liked from what I said I liked. Do you remember the day we played totem animals and I said yours was the llama? Well, mine was the chameleon. I made up my enthusiasm to suit my surroundings. [*Frankly*] You released me from all that. You gave me facts, ideas, reasons for things. You let me out of that hot, black burrow of feeling. I loved you then.

CHARLES [*dully*]: Then.

BELINDA: Yes.

CHARLES: But no longer?

[*A little pause.*]

BELINDA: I don't know. Living with you has taught me to respect my feelings – not alter them under pressure.

CHARLES: I'm not pressure.

BELINDA: Look, I know I was a pupil before. I admit it – it was good. But you were different then. Now I feel that you hate me half the time.

CHARLES: That's ridiculous.

BELINDA: Well, resent me, anyway. Like an awful headmaster. I feel I have to defend myself in front of you. I feel guilty.

CHARLES [*ironic*]: Do you? How extraordinary!

BELINDA: Charles, answer me something.

CHARLES: What?

BELINDA: Do you love me? I don't mean want me, for whatever reason. I mean, love me. Be honest.

CHARLES: Very much.

BELINDA: Then why the hell don't I feel it? 'I'm burning,' says the fire. But my cold hands say, 'No you're not.' Love with me is a great burst of joy that someone exists. Just that. Breathes! And with that joy comes a huge great need to go out and greet them. Yes, that's the word: *greet*. I used to greet you, inside me anyway, forty times a day. Now it's once a fortnight. And always when you're not looking. When you've got your hat on at an angle trying to look jaunty, which you can never manage anyway. It's all so dead with us now.

[*Pause.*]

CHARLES: And *he's* made you come alive?

BELINDA [*startled*]: What do you mean?

CHARLES: For someone who puts such a premium on her honesty, you make a pretty awful showing. I *know*, my dear. I *know*. So there's no need for any of this.

BELINDA: Know?

CHARLES: About him. Your man.

BELINDA: But you can't!...

CHARLES: But I do.

BELINDA: How?

CHARLES: Never mind how! I may be the pompous headmaster, but I'm not the village idiot. [*Pause.*] Don't you think you'd better tell me?

BELINDA: No.

CHARLES: Is it so painful?

BELINDA: It's not painful at all. But you just wouldn't dig it.

CHARLES: Give me the spade and let me try.

BELINDA: You're marvellous sometimes!

CHARLES: Thank you.

[*A pause. Husband and wife look at each other.*]

BELINDA: All right. I will. I will. Only you must promise not to interrupt.

CHARLES: Very well.

BELINDA: Just listen and make what sense of it you can.

CHARLES: All right.

BELINDA: I can make none, so we start equal.

CHARLES: Go on.

BELINDA: Well, you know I've been going out by myself for weeks.

CHARLES: I had noticed.

BELINDA: I was trying to think: that's all. Trying to pull myself out of the burrow on my own. I wandered about all over the place, it doesn't matter where. Then one day, about three weeks ago, a man sat down next to me on the bus, turned, and looked me straight in the eye. He was the most extraordinary man.

CHARLES: Handsome. Debonair. The look of a diplomat, no doubt.

BELINDA [*surprised*]: No, not at all like that. He was a goofy-looking man in a white raincoat, eating macaroons out of a polythene bag.

[CHARLES *gives her a startled look.*]

He had the funniest expression I ever saw – sort of witty – as if he wanted to wink, but didn't know how. At first I thought he was trying to pick me up, but it wasn't that. It took me a few minutes to work it out. What I was seeing was Approval. Simply that. Do you know, I'd forgotten what it was like to be looked at without criticism? I was so embarrassed I got up and left. He immediately got up too, and followed me. I began to walk very fast down Bond Street, and he walked just as fast behind, until we were both almost running. In the end I dived into the hairdressers and had quite an unnecessary shampoo. When I came out, he was waiting for me, leaning against Cartier's window, sucking an iced lolly. Since then we've been together every day. I don't expect you to believe what I'm going to tell you, but it's every word true.

CHARLES [*grimly*]: Go on, please.

BELINDA: You're getting upset, aren't you?

CHARLES: Never mind me. Just go on.

BELINDA: I don't want to upset you. I really don't.

CHARLES: On!

BELINDA: All right . . . First let me tell you the oddest thing about this whole affair. I call it an affair because it is one. But do you know, for the whole three weeks since we first saw each other, we haven't exchanged a single word? When I say we meet every day, I don't mean we make a date. All I mean is that like Mary's little lamb, wherever I go he's sure to follow. He's a pure genius at following. You never see him till he decides to show himself. Then he just pops up – click! Like that! – in a coffee bar or a cinema, or out from behind a statue in the Park. Once I turned round and there he was in the Powder Room at Fortnums! I suppose at the start I ought to have been scared, but I never was. Isn't that odd? All I knew was here was someone who approved of me. Who got pleasure out of just being in my company. Of course I realized he must be the loneliest man in town, but then in a way I was the loneliest girl, so it was sort of fitting. Who was I to complain if he got his kicks following me around? After a bit – and this is the really kooky thing – I began to get mine by following *him*.

CHARLES: What?

BELINDA: The day came when he took over. I'd stopped outside a cinema where there was a horror film, and looked back, as usual, just to make sure he'd seen me go in. And you know, he shook his head. He wasn't going to see that film! He was like you, you see: he didn't really like horror films. Mind you, he'd had a bit of a do with them: I'd made him sit through eleven that week. Instead he turned round, signed for me to follow and marched off to the next cinema. That was the first time I'd ever seen an Ingmar Bergman film. Charles, they're marvellous! This one has a poor old man driving all over Sweden in a motor car, looking for the turning he took wrong, years before. It's pathetic.

CHARLES: No doubt.

BELINDA: It is really. At one point he sees himself in his own coffin!

CHARLES: And this is all you've got to tell me?

BELINDA: Yes. Anyway, as far as what you're thinking's concerned. After that the whole thing became marvellous. We never knew what each day would bring. Sometimes I would lead. Sometimes he would. Last week I marched into the National Gallery and stopped in front of Bellini's portrait of a Doge. He was terribly grateful: you know, he'd obviously never seen it. He paid me back by leading me out to Syon House, which is hidden away behind all sorts of slummy things in Isleworth and has a huge hall of green marble, and eight statues life-size in gold! I know everything about him now: the things he likes doing, even what he likes to eat. They're all sweet things – he must be a Greek or something. Actually, he looks a bit Greeky. And he knows everything about me. The other day we were in a shop and he laid that out – [*She picks up the sombrero*] for me to buy. And it's the only hat I don't look stupid in.

CHARLES: Thank you.

BELINDA: Oh, Charles, it's not a question of hats. I've had the most intimate relationship of my life with someone I've never spoken to. What does it mean? . . . When I'm with him I live.

[CHARLES *stares at her with a numb expression on his face.*]

And because there aren't any words, everything's easy and possible. I share all the time. I share ... Actually, to be honest, I do feel guilty. I wasn't just passing. I wanted to talk to you. No, not talk. I knew that wouldn't be any good. I wanted to – I don't know – give you something. These flowers. Poor things – they look a bit withered, don't they? I'll get them some water.

[BELINDA *opens the office door, goes in – screams – and comes running back into the room. She is followed by* JULIAN *who stands blinking in the doorway. A pause.*]

CHARLES: Who on earth are *you*?

JULIAN [*surprised*]: My name is Cristoforou ...

CHARLES: I'm afraid the office is closed on Saturday mornings. If you'd care to make an appointment.

JULIAN: We've done that already.

CHARLES [*furious*]: What did I tell you to do?

JULIAN: Go down the fire escape into the mews.

CHARLES: Well?

JULIAN: I did, but the mews was so blank and abandoned. There was more life up here.

BELINDA: You know each other?

JULIAN: Your husband and I are new acquaintances. I don't think it will blossom beyond that.

CHARLES: How long have you been in there?

JULIAN: All the time. It was very illuminating. I mean you being so intimate. If you'd been discussing topics of general interest, I'd probably have gone away.

CHARLES: You mean you listened?

JULIAN: Of course. Eavesdropping is the second thing one is trained in, Mr Sidley. First shadow your man with your eye, then with your ear. It's an indispensable ability.

BELINDA: Charles, it's him!

JULIAN: He knows it is.

CHARLES: Don't.

JULIAN: I must.

BELINDA: Don't what?

CHARLES: No, please.

JULIAN: It's inevitable.

CHARLES: I forbid you to speak.

JULIAN: You can't. [*To* BELINDA] I think you should sit down.

BELINDA: Who are you?

CHARLES: I'm your employer. Leave this office at once!

BELINDA: Employer?

CHARLES: Do you hear?

BELINDA: Employer?

CHARLES: Please . . . I ask you as a friend.

JULIAN: You're not a friend.

BELINDA: Who are you? Tell me.

[*A pause.*]

JULIAN [*matter of factly*]: I am a private detective, Mrs Sidley. Hired by your husband to spy on you.

[*She stares at him in stunned amazement.*]

BELINDA [*faintly*]: No . . . [*She looks at her husband.*]

CHARLES: It was all I could think of to do. I was at my wits' end.

BELINDA: No. Oh, no!

CHARLES: I know it was awful. But what else could I do? Your behaviour was so odd. You must admit that. Any husband would have been suspicious.

BELINDA [*breaking out*]: No! No! No! No! NO!

CHARLES: Belinda –

BELINDA: Go away! You're filthy! Filthy! . . . I never want to see you again as long as I live!

[*She bursts into tears and collapses on the sofa, sobbing helplessly.* CHARLES *looks on impotently.*]

JULIAN: Well, you heard what she said. Go away.

CHARLES [*turning on him*]: What did you say?

JULIAN: I said go. It's what she wants.

CHARLES: You bloody meddling little wog! I'll teach you to make a fool out of me! Interfere with people's lives! . . .

[*He bounds forward, snatching up a ruler.* JULIAN *snatches up a heavy statuette and threatens him with it. He speaks in a new, sharp tone.*]

JULIAN: One step more, and I'll interfere with your brains –

[CHARLES *glares indecisively.*]

I mean it, Mr Sidley. Coshing is the third thing a detective's trained in.

[*Warily, breathing hard,* CHARLES *lowers the ruler.*]

That's better. Now, what have I done to upset you like this?

CHARLES: Only stolen my wife's affections, that's all!

JULIAN: Your wife's affections weren't stolen, Mr Sidley. They were going begging . . . [*Pause.*] And if you want them back, you must first learn how to get them. For a start, put down that ruler, and go out and walk around the gardens. It's time *you* waited for ten minutes.

[*When* JULIAN's *back is turned,* CHARLES *makes another attempt to hit him.* JULIAN *whirls round, statue in hand.*]

DO AS I SAY!

[*Even* BELINDA *is startled by this new tone of authority. Speechlessly,* CHARLES *looks from one to the other.*]

BELINDA: Oh Charles, for God's sake, just go!

[*With an attempt at dignity,* CHARLES *tucks the ruler under his arm and marches abruptly into the gardens. There is a pause.*]

JULIAN: So your name is Belinda.

BELINDA: Go away too.

JULIAN: Mine, as you may have heard, is Cristoforou. How strange it was to hear your voice for the first time! Even in a scream it sounded charming.

BELINDA: Go with him – go on. You're two of a kind.

JULIAN: You don't know my kind. It's very rare.

BELINDA: It's vile, that's all I know.

JULIAN: Why? What is my crime? The fairy tale Prince has turned back into a frog, is that it? Well, it's no fun for me either. I'd rather keep my magic. Though it's only training in how to shadow, you must admit I do it superbly. I should: I worked at it.

84

Surely you'd like to know why? It's a sad and fascinating story: the making of a detective.

BELINDA: I'm not listening.

JULIAN: Nonsense: you're riveted. Briefly, then, I am a middle-man. Most of my life has been spent making three where two are company. I was hardly out of puberty before I started becoming attracted to other men's wives. Women who were unattainable obsessed me. Usually, out of guilt, I'd work up a friendship with the husband, and take a painful pleasure in being a constant guest in their home. Masochism, you see: very un-Latin. I was always in the middle, getting nothing and being generally in the way. Finally I made myself so unhappy that I had to sit down and think. One day I asked myself this fateful question: 'Would you like to know a beautiful, tender, unattached girl to whom you were everything in the world?' And the answer came back: 'No!' ... Revelation! At that moment I realized something shattering about myself. I wasn't made to bear the responsibility of a private life! Obviously Nature never intended me to have one! I had been created to spend all my time in public! ... This thought simply delighted me. It seemed to account for everything – all the unhappiness I'd ever suffered. Alone, I didn't exist; I came alive only against a background of other people's affairs.

[*She turns and looks at him, fascinated.*]

Once I realized this, of course, it was the simplest thing in the world to select a permanent career. A detective was the obvious solution. I immediately resigned from Private Life, and became a Public Eye. A dick. Have a macaroon. They ease the heart.

BELINDA: Look: you've got no rights here, so why don't you just dick off to your dick's office?

JULIAN: Oh, how can you talk that to someone who's been as intimate with you as I have?

BELINDA: Intimate?

JULIAN: Do you deny we have spent three weeks in this city as blissfully as two people ever spent them in its history? Syon House!

The Isle of Dogs! Parliament Hill at six in the morning! Beware! There is no sin more unpardonable than denying you were pleased when pleasure touched you. You can die for that.

BELINDA: What the hell are you talking about?

JULIAN: You and I have exchanged our most personal treasures and that makes rights.

BELINDA: What rights? To make a fool of me?

JULIAN: Is that what I've done?

BELINDA: You know it is.

JULIAN: I don't. I found you aimless in London: I gave you direction. I found you smileless; I gave you joy. Not eternal joy, or even joy for a week. But immediate, particular, bright little minutes of joy – which is all we ever get or should expect. Give up self-pity. It doesn't become you.

BELINDA: Thanks for nothing!

JULIAN: And give up saying that too. It's hideous.

BELINDA: I'll say what I bloody want. It's no business of yours what I say.

JULIAN: Oh, but it is. You are my business. Look into my eye. Come on: look. No, this one.

[*Reluctantly she looks. He stares at her hypnotically, one inch from her face.*]

What do you see? I will tell you. You see one of the Seven Wonders of Nature. The completely Public Eye – which looks entirely outwards. Look into it. Beside this eye, the eagle is blind. The puma needs spectacles. Without immodesty I tell you – this eye possesses the most watchful iris, the most attentive cornea, the most percipient retina in the northern hemisphere. [*He suddenly withdraws it from her scrutiny.*] And for almost a month it has been focused exclusively on you. It has seen more in you than anyone you ever met, or ever will meet. Think of that. And, may I add, it belongs in the head of a man of taste and refinement who has been made to sit through more execrable horror films than anyone should be called on to see in a lifetime of duty! How dared you inflict on me

'Werewolves from Mars' *and* 'Bloodsuckers from Venus' both on
the same day? If that doesn't give me rights, what the hell does?

BELINDA: You're raving mad, aren't you? I should have realized it
all along.

JULIAN: It's not a word I can define, and your husband's books
aren't much help with it . . . [*He goes and looks through the window.*]
Look at him.

BELINDA: What's he doing?

JULIAN: Beheading the chrysanthemums with his ruler.

BELINDA: That's his way of working off anger. It's why I have to
buy all my flowers off barrows . . . He's always knocking the
dahlias about . . .

[*She starts to cry again. He hastens to her side, and sits down on the
sofa. She turns away.*]

JULIAN: Oh please, don't cry any more. I can't bear tears. They're
so excluding! Please! [*He takes her arm.*] Please. Let me dry your
eyes. [*Seductively.*] Belinda . . . [*Slowly she turns round.*] A simple
service from a simple friend. Eye-drying while you wait. Voilà!

[*He pulls out the handkerchief which is stuffed into his pocket at the
beginning of the play.* BELINDA *is showered with nuts and raisins.
Her crying turns to laughter.*]

I'm *agonized!* Utterly *agonized!* Did I hurt you? I'm sure I did.
Nothing can hurt more than a brazil nut aimed with force.
[BELINDA *begins to laugh really hard.*] And the carpet! Ohh! Look
at them – all over it!

[*He falls to his knees on the carpet and starts picking up the raisins
and popping them in his mouth as he talks.*]

And such a *gorgeous rug!* Real Bokhara! I can tell. I used to sell
them once, door to door, wearing a fez and a stick-on goatee.
Some dreadful gimmick of my employers. I looked like an extra
out of 'Kismet' and sold nothing at all *ever*, not even a welcome mat.

[*She stops laughing. He offers her a raisin from the floor.*]

Would you like one?

BELINDA: Your need is greater than mine!

JULIAN [*seriously*]: Will you give me one more minute before you throw me out?

BELINDA: Well?

[*He squats cross-legged in front of her.*]

JULIAN: Look: this is my last day as a private detective. After your husband gets through with me, I can't hope to go back to Mayhew and Figgis, or anybody else. It's just as well. I was on the point of resigning anyway. You can't imagine how wretched the job is. How unworthy.

BELINDA: I thought you loved it.

JULIAN: I thought I would, too. But I reckoned without my awful desire to be liked. Well, if you're a dick you can't be. If you give your employer bad news he hates you. If you give him good he thinks his money's been wasted. Either way you can't win.

BELINDA: Well, I don't see how I can help.

JULIAN: Oh, but you can. You can get me back my self-respect.

BELINDA: Me?

JULIAN: Yes, Belinda. I've spent three years helping to break up people's marriages. Don't you think it might make it up to them a little if I helped to preserve yours? Let me be honest with you: I'd like to be the first detective to *cement* a marriage.

BELINDA: That's a lovely thought, but I'm not going to stay with Charles to oblige you.

JULIAN: Why not? You owe me something. You made me betray a job which I've never done in my whole life before.

BELINDA: *I* did?

JULIAN: Certainly. I was paid to follow you, not sit down beside you on a bus.

BELINDA: Why did you, then?

JULIAN: I couldn't help it. You're a witch. You can throw an acorn at a duck and strike the heart of a man with grief at fifty paces. I knew it as soon as ever I saw you, standing all alone in the mists of Hyde Park. There was something about your loneliness that filled my eyes with tears! I tasted at a distance the salt of your solitude! After a week of following you about, staring aimlessly into windows, crumbling endless filthy cakes in endless loathsome coffee-bars, I did something which my whole training was powerless to prevent. I sat down beside you in a bus, and smiled. Your hand, Belinda! Darkness shades me! On thy bosom let me rest! ... I quote as you may imagine.

BELINDA: Look, there are limits to humouring the mad, and I've reached them.

JULIAN: You love your husband. You admitted it to him before. Or at least all your wish is to find your way to him.

BELINDA: Oh stop!

JULIAN: What?

BELINDA: All that magaziny language.

JULIAN: I've got a magaziny mind. You've found me out. I should never have talked. When I was dumb we understood each other.

BELINDA: If there's any finding ways back to be done, it's by him – not me. If you'd known him as he was you'd have adored him. He used to be gay – really gay. He used to say hundreds of funny things and then laugh at them himself, which I think's a marvellous sign, to laugh at your own jokes. It means you're *in* life. Now he's sort of out of it, sarcastic and gritty, as if something's drying him up.

JULIAN: It is.

BELINDA: What?

JULIAN: Jealousy.

BELINDA: Jealousy? If anyone should be jealous it's me!

JULIAN: What d'you mean by that?

BELINDA: Nothing.

JULIAN: You mean he's unfaithful to you?

BELINDA: Oh no, not really. He takes himself off to a tart sometimes, somewhere in Ladbroke Grove. That's not really unfaithful. He'd die of shame if he thought I knew.

JULIAN: How *do* you know?

BELINDA: A friend of mine saw him going in one day. Her name's

Madame Conchita, which is a lovely name for a tart, isn't it? I mean, you can just see her. Sort of Bayswater Brazilian! He must have found her in the Ladies' Directory.

JULIAN: What on earth's that?

BELINDA: A sort of underground directory of tarts. Privately published. Charles is riveted by it. He keeps a copy in his desk. I found it there one day.

JULIAN: Oh, you poor thing.

BELINDA: Not at all. It served me right for prying.

JULIAN: And you're not jealous?

BELINDA: Of course not. I think it's very sensible of him. Men should have a change from their wives occasionally. It makes for a happy home.

JULIAN: I haven't noticed it in your case.

BELINDA: Neither have I. What do you mean, he's jealous? What's he jealous of?

JULIAN [gravely]: All your personal life which he hasn't given you. When you married, you were his pupil. He talked, you listened. Then one day as, you said, school closed. The chameleon began to change into a princess. Your own thoughts sprouted and you turned into yourself. That's what he can't forgive: your life outside of him. It's not really unusual. Many husbands want to create wives in their own image: they allow a certain growth – so far and no farther. Thereafter they will resent all changes they haven't caused, all experiences they haven't shared, and – with wives brighter than they – all new things they can't keep up with.

BELINDA: But I'm not brighter than Charles.

JULIAN: Oh, Belinda – a million times!

BELINDA [astonished]: Me?

JULIAN: Of course. Do you want to know what I think about your Charles?

BELINDA: What?

JULIAN: I think he's pitiful.

BELINDA: He isn't!

JULIAN: He's so afraid of being touched by life, he hardly exists.

He's so scared of looking foolish, he puts up words against it for barriers: Good Taste, Morality. What you *should* do, what you *should* feel. He's walled up in Should like a tomb.

BELINDA: What a marvellous comparison!

JULIAN: It's true, isn't it?

BELINDA: I suppose it is. Poor Charles.

JULIAN: Lucky Charles, to have you. Because he's sick and you're well.

BELINDA: He's not sick! He's just a bit stuffy, that's all.

JULIAN: Sick. If you hear a piece of music, you'll either love it or hate it. He won't know what to feel till he knows who it's by. Sick. You can say 'nigger' and have black friends. He'll only say 'negro' – but dislike them.

BELINDA: That's true.

JULIAN: Sick.

BELINDA [*eagerly*]: Go on! More!

JULIAN: You're Spirit, Belinda, and he's Letter. You've got passion where all he's got is pronouncement.

BELINDA: You're not mad. You're not mad at all. You don't miss anything.

JULIAN: Of course. I have a Public Eye.

BELINDA: What else does it see?

JULIAN: That Charles Sidley is half-dead, and only his wife can save him.

BELINDA: How? What can I do?

JULIAN: You're a witch. You can do anything. Don't you know what you did for me?

BELINDA: What?

JULIAN: You gave me a private life. For three weeks I walked through London, all alone except for you, to point the way. And slowly, for the first time since I can remember, I began to feel my own feelings. In the depths of that long silence I began to hear the rustle of my own emotions growing. At first just one or two little shoots, quick to die – then thicker, stronger – my very own feelings, Belinda, my very own reactions! And I was no longer

91

displaced. *I was the being who contained this rustling.* You talked about burrows of feeling without thought. But there's something worse: burrows of not feeling anything. Burrows of deadness! Burrows of numbness! Burrows of sleep and torpor where you hide away from experience because you are afraid of changing! Like him. Clinging to a past self that festers when it's clung to. [*He takes her hand.*] You led me out of those burrows, Belinda. Now lead him the same way. Eurydice leading Orpheus for a change.

BELINDA: Who were they?

JULIAN: Lovers who found their way back from Hades by not looking at each other. Only you do it by not speaking which is so much better in this babel we're all in. How many more people would stay married if they just shut up, and listened, and heard each other's heartbeats in the daytime?

[*A pause. They look at one another. He kisses her hand.*]

You gave me the only gift I really needed. Now give it to him.

BELINDA: How?

JULIAN: The same way. In silence.

BELINDA: You mean not speak to him?

JULIAN: Of course. It's his only chance.

BELINDA: But that's impossible! –

JULIAN [*excited*]: Of course! Of course! Of course! [*He goes quickly to the window. Calling.*] Mr Sidley! Yes, you! Come up here at once!

BELINDA: What are you going to do?

JULIAN: Do you trust me?

BELINDA: No!

JULIAN: Do you want to return to your marriage?

BELINDA: Yes, I do.

JULIAN: Then do exactly as I say. Do you promise?

BELINDA: I don't know why I should.

JULIAN: Put yourself completely under my orders for a month. I promise in return it'll work.

BELINDA: For a month?

JULIAN: Unavoidable. Promise.

BELINDA: A month's forever.

JULIAN: It's four weeks. Promise.

BELINDA: And I think you really are mad after all.

JULIAN: Promise.

BELINDA: Yes.

JULIAN: You break it and you'll go to hell. Stand there. When he comes in, don't look at him! And whatever happens don't speak.

BELINDA: Don't speak?

JULIAN: Not a single word.

BELINDA: That's idiotic.

JULIAN: Are you questioning me?

BELINDA: Yes!

JULIAN: Oh well, then, the game's off. There's no fun playing Master and Slave if you're going to question everything.

BELINDA: No, I'm sorry. I'll behave. But not speaking is a bit brutal. You forget I'm a woman.

JULIAN: Well, you'd better get used to it. You're going to have to do it for thirty days.

[*She opens her mouth in surprise.*]

Ssh. Here he comes. Stand up straight. Look proud!

[BELINDA *stands like a statue.* CHARLES *comes storming in.*]

CHARLES: Well, who are *you* shouting at?

JULIAN: You.

CHARLES: Belinda, I think it's time we went home, don't you? We can discuss all this later, at home. Are you coming, dear? [*Pause.*] Belinda, I'm talking to you. [*Pause.*] I'd like you to come home now, do you hear?

JULIAN: It isn't any good, is it, Mr Sidley?

CHARLES [*angrily*]: Belinda!

JULIAN: It's useless to address her. She will not reply. As far as you are concerned, she has renounced speech. I bear her exact and peremptory ultimatum. She is so shattered by your conduct – setting a low, sneaking, prying little wog of a detective spy on her – that she is leaving you forever.

CHARLES: Belinda!

[BELINDA *turns to protest, but is gestured to keep silent by* JULIAN.]

JULIAN: Unless. Yes, you are lucky. There's an Unless. You have one chance of keeping her. But only one. That is – you will take my place in the streets of London. [*Formally*] You will follow her every day for a month, at a distance of fifty feet, wherever she chooses to go. You will look at whatever she chooses to point at. You will hear whatever she chooses to listen to. You will sit, stand, skip, slide, or shuffle entirely at her will. And for all this month, neither in study nor street, at table nor in bed, will you exchange a single word. [*More easily*] If there's anything special you want to see and show her, then you may lead. But it had better be good. This is your will, isn't it, Belinda?

[BELINDA *nods.*]

Inexorable, aren't you, Belinda? The alternative is divorce.

[*Nod.*]

Sunderment!

[*Nod.*]

Eternal separation!

CHARLES: Are you done?

JULIAN: Oh yes. End of words, start of action. [*To* BELINDA, *taking her hand.*] Go forth, Eurydice!

CHARLES: Stay here, Belinda!

[*A long pause.* BELINDA *looks between the two men, choosing. Then she smiles at* JULIAN, *picks up her hat and starts to walk out.*]

JULIAN: I suggest the Michelangelo Coffee Bar for a start. Make him eat a Leaning Tower of Pisa.

CHARLES: Belinda?

JULIAN: No, make him eat two!

[BELINDA *goes.* CHARLES *follows her to the door.*]

CHARLES: This seems a good joke to you, but what are you really doing? You're acting on impulse, that's all. [*He is now out of sight.*] You're living on pure emotion without thought or ... Belinda ... Belinda! ... Belinda? [CHARLES *comes back, slamming door.*] If she thinks I'm going after her, she's mad.

94

JULIAN: I strongly advise you to follow her, Mr Sidley.

CHARLES: Do you? Do you indeed? Well fortunately you don't know my wife as well as you think. She'll get tired of this nonsense in an hour. Now get out. And I may as well tell you I'm going to see to it immediately that you are fired.

JULIAN: I'm agonized. Actually I have a much better job to go to.

CHARLES: Indeed?

JULIAN: Yes. Yours. I've come to a decision. While you are outside doing my job, I'll sit here and do yours. Exchange is no robbery, as they say. And even if it is, robbery can be rather stimulating.

CHARLES: Very humorous.

JULIAN: It may well be. I've always had a hankering after the accountant's life. [*Pompous voice*] 'Good morning, Miss Smith: bring me the Sidley Trust file, please.' 'My dear sir, you have made a great deal of money. You must look to pay a great deal of tax. However, there are one or two – what can one say? – loopholes, I believe, is the vulgar word. I prefer "modes of avoidance".'

CHARLES: If you are not out of this office in one minute by my watch, I shall call the police.

JULIAN: If you are not out of this office in thirty seconds by my watch –

CHARLES: Well?

JULIAN: I shall tell your wife about Ladbroke Grove.

CHARLES [*startled*]: What did you say?

JULIAN: I'm not a private detective for nothing, Mr Sidley. And I did give you warning I was a good one. Once I was sure of your wife's innocence, I took to wondering about yours. So I followed you.

CHARLES: I don't believe it.

JULIAN [*lightly*]: Madame Conchita? . . . Olé! . . . Not exactly my type. We wogs prefer something more Home Counties. Let's see . . . There ought to be reference books on the subject. And I'm sure your superb collection must contain at least one encyclopedia on matters sexual. One Almanac of Arcana? At the very least, a Directory.

CHARLES [*his voice faltering*]: Directory?

JULIAN: Perhaps it's in the Pornographic Selection.

[*He moves towards the office door.* CHARLES *puts himself between him and it.*]

Ah, closed to the general public.

CHARLES: How dare you?

JULIAN: Go through your desk? Routine procedure. You have fifteen seconds, Mr Sidley. [*He takes out of his bag a large grapefruit and knife and the canister of sugar.*] Look: as I told you. I never fail jobs, they always fail me. I can hold the fort here perfectly well for a month. I'll just sit here, turn all comers into Corporations, and let them enjoy themselves. To be an accountant nowadays you simply need a highly developed sense of fantasy. And I'm sure you'll admit I've got that. [*He slices through the grapefruit and puts it into a glass ashtray. The telephone rings.*] Hello? No, this is Mr Sidley's assistant.

[CHARLES *makes a grab for the telephone, but* JULIAN *dodges.*]

He's on holiday for a month. That's right: one month. [*As* CHARLES *makes another effort to grab it*] One moment please. [*He puts down the telephone, and shoves the open receiver in a drawer. He looks very seriously at* CHARLES.] Look, my dear man, don't be entirely stupid. Your wife's failing love may not be a deductible expense – but it's the only thing you've got.

[*A pause.* CHARLES *returns his stare, tacitly admitting the truth of this. He lowers his eyes.*]

[*As if to a child*] Go on. Or you'll lose her. [*Indicating the white raincoat*] And put that on. It may help. Conditioned reflex, you know. If you find any goodies in it, you're very welcome to them.

[*Stunned,* CHARLES *obeys.* JULIAN *sits at the desk.*]

Remember: one month. I do know your wife, Mr Sidley, and I know she'll keep at it. But if, by any small chance, she wavers, you must insist. Otherwise – Madame Conchita! . . . Go on, now.

[*He watches, smiling amiably, as* CHARLES *retreats to the door.*] I'll have the bill sent here, of course. It's more discreet, isn't it?

CHARLES [*viciously*]: One thing, Mr Cristoforou. If I may remind you, you said that the man my wife met every day was handsome, well dressed, Mr Cristoforou. Debonair.

JULIAN: So I did, Mr Sidley. So I did. I thought it more tactful. I mean any husband can be excused for losing out to a dream figure like that. But to someone like me? . . . [*Taking the receiver from the drawer.*] Hello? Sorry to have kept you waiting. Yes, he felt the need for a complete rest. [*Pointedly at* CHARLES] Yes, he had to *go*!

[CHARLES *goes.*]

Well, permit me to introduce myself. My name is Cristoforou. Julian Cristoforou. Diplomas in Accountancy from the Universities of Cairo, Beirut, Istanbul and Damascus, Author of the well-known handbook 'Teach Yourself Tax Evasion'. What seems to be your particular problem? Income tax? . . . Yes? It's monstrous! You haven't paid it, I hope? I'm delighted to hear it. Of course not. Paying any tax that is more than one per cent of your total income I consider a desperate imprudence. Yes, of course, we have limitless experience in this field. Cristoforou and Sidley. A firm of the very highest. I think you'd better come round and see me immediately. [*He eats the grapefruit: it is obviously sour. He shakes the canister of sugar: it is obviously empty.*] No, my dear sir, I assure you, we won't let the Government touch a penny piece of your money. Not without a battle that will make the Battle of Waterloo look like a scuffle on the village green. Come round in, shall we say one hour? I look forward to it. In the meantime, don't worry about a thing. And if you could bring round with you a pound of granulated sugar, I'd be greatly obliged. Good-bye to you, sir. Good-bye! [*He hangs up as –*

THE CURTAIN FALLS

WHITE LIARS

A PLAY IN ONE ACT

FOR
MY PARENTS
WITH LOVE

CHARACTERS

SOPHIE, BARONESS LEMBERG

FRANK

TOM

WHITE LIARS

The Fortune Teller's Parlour of SOPHIE, BARONESS LEMBERG, *on the pier of a run-down seaside resort on the south coast of England. Around 5 p.m., late September.*

SOPHIE'S *parlour is set between two levels of the pier. It is reached from above by an iron staircase, and it is set on iron stanchions rising out of the sea. As we look at it, it seems to be suspended against the wet five o'clock sky; a cluttered nest in a tangle of Victorian ironwork. The room is actually divided by a curtain into two: a little ante-room, with a bench for waiting; and the consulting-room, which is much larger, and is replete with a covered table on a rotting strip of carpet, and a couple of broken-down chairs. On the table stands the faded photograph of a middle-aged man, in an ornate silver frame. A completed game of patience is laid out on the cloth. On a shelf at the back stands the crystal ball, under a covering. The window, streaked with salt and bird-droppings, proclaims in reverse gilt letters:* Baroness Lemberg. Palmist. Clairvoyante. *And in smaller letters underneath:* Lemberg Never Lies. *The place is dirty and claustrophobic, deriving its mystery from the fantasy of its location, hung over the water. Little light bulbs are festooned down the pier, above.*

[*As the curtain rises and the lights come up through the cobweb of rusty iron, we see* SOPHIE *standing at her table, carefully pouring gin from a half-bottle through a funnel into a rose-coloured decanter. She is a woman of fifty, once beautiful and still handsome, dressed in the blouse and skirt of a professional working woman. When she speaks her voice is marked by a strong but never incomprehensible German accent. She drops the bottle into a waste-basket, picks up a delicate little rose-coloured wineglass and pours some gin into it. Seagulls suddenly scream. She raises her glass to them.*]

SOPHIE: *Salut!* Bloody things! Greedy, filthy, middle-class birds. Here's to you! And to another brilliant, dazzling afternoon in Grinmouth-on-Sea! Grinmouth, glorious Grinmouth – Fairyland of the South Coast! [*She swallows her gin.*] You know something, I think they're watering the drink in this country. This is definitely less fortifying than it used to be. But that of course is no surprise. It is one of the iron laws of life: everything gets less fortifying. What Goes Down Must Go Downer! Lemberg's Law of Life . . .! [*She turns to the photograph. Imploringly, like a little girl*] Oh, don't look so disapproving, please. What else am I going to do? Improve my mind for the glittering society of Grinmouth-on-Sea? Look at it! [*She goes to the window.*] Not one gleam of sunlight for ten days. Not one soul out walking, jetty to jetty. Nothing but wet sand – rusty iron – plastic bottles all along the shore, and bird-shit on the windows. I'm sorry for the language, Papa, but there it is: see for yourself. *Vogeldrecke* on every pane; who needs curtains? And the sea. This ravishing sea! Look at it, if you please – such an exotic colour. It's exactly like they've poured out ten million cups of tea. No wonder they call it the English Channel! Grinmouth-on-*Tea*, that's what I name it from now on. [*She laughs sourly.*] You hear that, Papa? That's my joke for today. Grinmouth-on-Tea! I admit it's not one of my best. But then *you* sit here all day entirely by yourself, you're not going to win decorations for your wit either! [*She pours some more gin, and gulps.*] The truth is, my dear, they haven't the faintest idea what water should look like in this country. Do you remember our lake? Our beautiful summer lake, what it was like to come back to each year? Clear, clear water – absolutely still – with the pine-trees standing in it, upside down – how was it you called them? – rows of little green soldiers marching on their heads! You had really a good power of description, you know, sometimes . . . [*She sits at her table.*] Beloved God, this silence! You'd think *someone* would consult me, if only to ask should they kill themselves. Do you realize there hasn't been an actual human being in this room for six days? And then it was only Mr Fowler with his boring rent book. [*Imitating a 'common' accent*] 'I hate to mention it, Baroness, but you owe us more than a little back rent!' More than a little! Only six bloody weeks! 'Hate to mention it' – he loves it; boring old swine! Sorry, Papa, your Sophie is getting just a little bad-tempered with the world. Can you really blame her? How would *you* like it to sit here all day in this black little prison, with draughts going up *your* skirts. I'm sorry, I mean trousers! [*She giggles.*] Excuse me, Father – you are absolutely right. A lady shouldn't drink. Though actually, I don't know why. I was under the impression, my dear, that the aristocracy *set* the dos and don'ts, not followed them. That is entirely for the middle classes ... [*She looks up and out.*] Beloved God, I don't believe it! –

[FRANK *and* TOM *appear on the upper level.*]

Two whole clients! Oh God, oh my God! ...

[FRANK *and* TOM *lounge down the iron stairs and stand outside her window, apparently debating whether to come in. She watches them hungrily.*]

Two pounds if they take the cards. Four if they take the crystal ball! Beloved God, make them come in!

[*The two boys start to walk away.*]

Come in, oh *please*!

[*They turn back and enter the ante-room.*]

TOM: Anyone home?

SOPHIE: One moment, please!

[*She scurries about during the following, stacking the cards, getting the crystal ball and setting it on the table, and adjusting her hair. Finally, she swirls around herself a coloured shawl, sits and opens a fan! Of the two boys,* FRANK *is middle-class, soft-spoken and gentle; his manner is shy, warm, and immediately likeable – in great contrast to his companion, who seems casual almost to the point of brutality.* TOM *is dressed very 'trendily', in bright colours, wears his hair long, and slumps about. He speaks in a heavy North Country accent.*]

FRANK: I'll go first.

TOM: Why?

FRANK: I've got to get back to the Hall. I want to check that sound system.

TOM: Why bother? There's not going to be an audience anyway.

FRANK: And whose fault is that?

TOM: What d'you mean?

FRANK: We wouldn't be here at all, if it wasn't for your stupid astrologer.

TOM: He's not stupid.

FRANK: 'Avoid the seaside in the month of August.' What d'you call *that*?

TOM: Don't mock what you don't understand.

FRANK: All right, all right. I don't know what I'm doing with you anyway. You don't need a business manager. Why not just hire yourself a crack astrologer, and get him to fix all your engagements for you? He could make sure we'd go broke inside a month.

TOM [*surly*]: Shut up, will you?

FRANK: What are you going to ask *her* now? Where we play next?

TOM: I said, Shut up. OK?

FRANK [*appeasingly*]: Look, Tom – I'm not mocking. You've got a right to believe what you please. But really this – this stuff can go too far sometimes. A two-year-old baby could tell you you don't play the seaside in late bloody September. If we'd come here six weeks ago, when they *wanted* us, we'd have cleaned up, and you know it.

SOPHIE [*calling*]: Come in, please!

FRANK: I'm sorry but that's the truth. Astrology or no astrology!

[TOM *brushes by him into the consulting-room.* FRANK *follows him quickly.* SOPHIE *is seated regally at her table.*]

SOPHIE: Good evening. One of you at a time, please.

TOM [*dismissing* FRANK]: Right. I'll see you, then.

FRANK [*standing his ground*]: I – well, why don't we toss for it?

TOM [*surprised at being challenged*]: Toss?

FRANK: Well, that's fair, isn't it?

[TOM *shrugs sullenly.* FRANK *pulls a coin from his pocket.*]

Well, it is ... [*To* SOPHIE, *with a nervous laugh*] We're both so anxious to see you, it's a bit of a fight. [*To* TOM] Heads or tails?

TOM: Heads.

[FRANK *tosses.*]

FRANK: Tails! I win! [*Showing it to* SOPHIE] True?

[SOPHIE *nods in acquiescence.*]

[*To Tom*] Look, why don't you go for a ride on the dodgems? They'll be glad of the custom.

[TOM *shrugs again.*]

SOPHIE: Come back in ten minutes, please. Expert divination does not take very long.

FRANK: You don't mind, do you?

TOM: You won, didn't you?

[TOM *lounges out, upstairs and out of sight.* FRANK *looks after him.*]

SOPHIE: Come along, then.

FRANK [*staring out of the window*]: It's a rotten old day, isn't it? There isn't a soul out on the prom. Just us and the seagulls. They're all sitting in those little shelters meant for people.

SOPHIE: Like rows of people from a sanitarium, coughing into their coat collars.

FRANK: That's a nasty thought.

SOPHIE: It's a nasty place, mister. It makes you have nasty ideas.

[*He turns to look at her.*]

FRANK: It must feel strange living with the sea all around you.

SOPHIE: It is not a sea at all. It is merely a gutter between here and France. All the same, I prefer it to the land. A third-rate holiday resort is not my idea of a place to reside in ... I have known other days, mister.

FRANK: I'd assumed that, of course.

SOPHIE: You had? Why?

FRANK: From your manner. It's very – distinguished. And also of course from – well, your title.

SOPHIE: I am a Baroness of the Holy Roman Empire. I was born with certain powers. Owing to an alteration in my fortune, I am reduced to selling these for money. It is regrettable, but then so is most of contemporary life . . . You have a special purpose in coming to see me. Please tell me what it is, and don't waste my time.

FRANK: A special purpose?

SOPHIE: Of course.

FRANK: How do you know?

SOPHIE: That wasn't tails, mister.

FRANK: What?

SOPHIE: The coin. It wasn't tails. It was heads.

FRANK [grinning nervously]: Oh . . . Yes, yes – yes – that's right. I know. I'm sorry about that. But I – I – I had to see you first. I really had . . . It's vital.

SOPHIE: Ja?

FRANK [very ill at ease]: When we drove into town this morning in the van, I saw your sign right away. It says 'Advice and Consultation'. It sort of gave me the idea. Well, it gave me hope, actually.

SOPHIE: Go on.

FRANK: I don't know. It seemed like a good idea, then. Now it's perfectly ridiculous. I mean, just embarrassing, really . . . The thing is, you mustn't be angry.

SOPHIE: Angry?

FRANK: At what I'm going to ask. Promise that, please, You see, I've – I've got a suggestion. A sort of a – little game. A well, frankly a . . . Look, Baroness, I don't really want my fortune told at all. I've come about something entirely different. And you've every right to throw me out, and be very annoyed. Only I hope you won't be.

SOPHIE: Young mister: I have no idea what you are saying. Am I supposed to be clairvoyant, or something? That's my joke. I often make it.

FRANK: Oh . . . Yes . . .

SOPHIE: Sit down for a start. Come – come.

[FRANK *sits.*]

You're very pale. Are you ill?

FRANK: No.

SOPHIE: Worried?

FRANK: Yes.

SOPHIE: Is it your professional life?

FRANK. No. Look, I'll pay you, just like it was a regular session. Actually, I thought I'd offer you a little more. Unless you'd be insulted.

SOPHIE: Why should I be insulted? Advice is as hard as divination. It is your love life? Trouble with a girl? Ha?

[FRANK *shrugs.*]

Of course. And your friend is involved also, Ja, ja, ja . . .

FRANK: A bit cliché, isn't it?

SOPHIE: It is not exactly unfamiliar, I admit. Two friends in love with the same girl.

FRANK: Except he's *not* in love with her. And she just thinks she's in love with him. She's very easily impressed. Mind you, I see in a way. He's an impressive boy. Susan's always been surrounded by phonies. Suddenly, along comes someone who's completely himself – it's bound to be a turn-on.

SOPHIE: A what?

FRANK: It's bound to excite her.

SOPHIE: This boy is working-class, ja?

FRANK: He could hardly be more so.

SOPHIE: And the girl is not?

FRANK: You're clever, Baroness. You see things. Sue's bugbear is respectability. Her dad is a nice respectable department manager in John Lewis's. He's got himself a nice, respectable house in Chislehurst, and she's had enough golf and gardening to last her a lifetime. Tom represents everything her parents hate. Rotten slum background. Independence of the kind that really makes them nervous. The kind you can only have when you've truly had nothing to begin with. They'd call it arrogance. Well, you've seen him. He *is* arrogant, of course, he is. He's also extraordinary. [*Pause.*] The trouble with me is, I see everyone's point of view. Here I am, defending him already.

SOPHIE: This boy is an entertainer?

FRANK: Singer. Thanks to me. I found him singing in an East End pub, flat broke. A natural musician. I mean really marvellous. And with absolutely no idea what to do with it. I made a whole Group for him. That's my thing, you see: I'm a manager, no point in being modest about it. If he's a natural singer, I'm a natural manager. I created the Liars especially for him.

SOPHIE: The Liars?

FRANK: The White Liars. Four instrumentalists and Tom. I even designed the uniform. White satin - it's wild! Susan helped me, of course.

SOPHIE: She helps you a lot, your girl?

FRANK: I don't know what I'd do without her. She does everything. Drives the van, does the accounts, nursemaids the boys - you'll meet her tonight, if you like. We're doing a show at the Winter Garden. Perhaps you'd like to come.

SOPHIE: Thank you, no. As far as I'm concerned, the birth of electricity meant the death of music.

FRANK [*laughing politely*]: That's good.

SOPHIE: It's not good, mister. It's true. There is no music made today: just noise.

FRANK: If you say so, Baroness.

SOPHIE: Don't condescend to me, please. I come from the one country that created all the music that matters! And I was brought up to *listen* to it, my dear mister. Not just bob my head, or twist my tummy. My father was a *real* natural musician! He was an *amateur* in the true meaning of the word. Do you know what that means? A lover! He played the clarinet like a lover! It is hard to appreciate amateurs in the other sense of the word - bricklayers and plumbers hitting guitars - when one has known the Rosé.

FRANK: Rosé?

SOPHIE: The Rosé String Quartet. No doubt you've never heard of them. Before the war they were the finest chamber players in Austria. My father knew them intimately. He would invite them each summer to our villa in the country, to play with him. And they would come. 'Sir,' they'd say, 'it is an honour to play with someone as good as you!' They would all sit by the lake, by this glorious lake on our beautiful little private estate, and they would play together – the Brahms Quintet, in B Minor. I would always be the guest of honour. Ten, eleven, twelve years old, they'd put me in the middle of them, on a special armchair carried out on to the grass, and I would sit *engulfed* in the music! Sentimental, ja? Well, other years – other tears.

FRANK: It sounds marvellous.

SOPHIE: My father was a man of great style. It is a way of conduct that has passed entirely from the world.

FRANK [*looking at the photograph*]: Is that him there?

SOPHIE: It is.

FRANK: What are those things he's wearing?

SOPHIE [*loftily: not looking at the picture herself*]: You mean decorations. The top one is the Order of St Michael. Next the Golden Spur. Last the papal medal of the Holy Roman Empire. Impressive, ja? As you would say – wow!

FRANK: Is he still alive?

SOPHIE: No. He drowned.

FRANK: Drowned?

SOPHIE: Ja: in middle-class mediocrity. When the Nazis came, we left Austria. What else could we do? As he observed, no man of civilization could continue to live there. Besides, my mother was of Romany blood. It was from her I derive my gift. Her mother had been a noblewoman of that very ancient race – but of course to the Nazis the Romanys were simply degenerates. We lived together all three in London. My father tried to work, but he'd been trained for nothing practical. All his life he'd been a diplomat – and the new government detested him. The Third Reich only had use for traitors, of course. And so he passed his time mostly sitting by himself in Regent's Park, reading music scores, whilst first my mother and then I, after she'd taught me properly, practised our gift of divination . . . Other years, other tears. We were talking of your girl friend. What is it you want of me? You love her, ja?

FRANK: Yes.

SOPHIE: Very much?

FRANK: We've been together two years – and it's been the best time I've ever known.

SOPHIE: But now it is ending?

FRANK: Not if I can help it.

SOPHIE: Because of him? Your friend?

FRANK: Look, when I first met Tom he'd only been down from Yorkshire three weeks. He was living in a filthy little cellar in the slums. He was absolutely miserable.

SOPHIE: So you took him into your house?

FRANK: The stupidest thing I ever did. I gave him a room in my flat, free. The thing about Tom is, he's a monster, I mean that in the Greek way. Like one of those things in a fable. He *lives* on worship. It's his food. I mean it quite literally: he can hardly get through a day without two tablespoons of sticky golden worship poured down his throat, preferably by a girl. Poor Sue walked right into it, you see. I mean because that's a bit her scene – spooning it out. And the awful thing is, she's getting more and more turned on. Every day I watch it happening. It's like I can't stop it. Any moment now she's going to cross that landing from our bedroom to his. I just know it.

SOPHIE: So prevent it! Tell him to go!

FRANK: Well, that's it. I can't – I just can't. I'm just – incapable. Isn't that stupid? . . . For one thing, it's just so corny – Keep Your Hands Off My Girl! I mean he'd laugh. I'd just look so silly, you know, squaring up . . . It's not me. Anyway, it isn't that simple. The thing is – he's so bloody disarming. I can't explain really. I lie in bed at night beside her, rehearsing scenes I'm going to have with Tom in the morning. I make up whole conversations – brilliant cutting sentences – or maybe ones more in sorrow than in anger, you know – rather noble. And then in the daylight I look at him and he's swabbing crusts round the egg yolk on his plate, and I just can't bring them out. I mean, people aren't in your head, are they? [*Pause.*] The thing is, I can't take any more. He's got to get out! *I've got to get him out!*

    [*His vehemence seems to surprise them both.*]

    [*After a pause*] I had this wild idea.

SOPHIE: What kind of idea?

FRANK: That you could – see it all.

SOPHIE: See?

FRANK: In the ball.

SOPHIE [*slowly*]: See all – what?

FRANK [*getting nervous*]: Look, the thing about Tom is – he's fantastically superstitious. I mean, ridiculous. He's always loping off to fortune-tellers and palmists, every place he goes. One week it's a woman in Acton, who does it with beans. The next, it's some Chinaman in Clapham who does it with dice.

SOPHIE: And now it's some German in Grinmouth who does it – with what exactly?

FRANK: Well, this, actually, I thought . . . [*He produces an envelope from his pocket.*] The main facts of Tom's life. It's all stuff he's told me over the past year. Yorkshire childhood – coal-mining village – drunken dad who threw his guitar on the fire. They're pretty dismal, really. I thought –

SOPHIE: What? That as I'm a fake, I could not possibly find them out for myself?

FRANK: Of course not! Only using this, you'd be absolutely accurate. I mean absolutely. So exact you'd have him freaked. He'd totally believe you – totally: you can't imagine it. I mean if you were to see something a bit . . .

SOPHIE: Ja? A bit . . .?

FRANK: Alarming – in his future.

SOPHIE [*carefully*]: What kind of alarming, mister?

FRANK: Well, like some dangerous relationship.

SOPHIE: With a girl.

FRANK: Yes.

SOPHIE: Which, of course, he should break off immediately. If he doesn't terrible disaster waits for him. Ja? [*Amused*] Blood and calamity!

FRANK: It sounds ridiculous, I know. Like I said. With anyone else but Tom it would be. But I swear to you, any kind of warning coming from you – because you're very impressive, you really are – he'd actually stop and think. It could work.

SOPHIE: And how much am I to receive for this absurdity?

FRANK: I thought five pounds would be . . .

SOPHIE: Suitable? [*Silence.*] Mister, I know I don't look so prosperous here in this filthy little room, but who do you think I am? Some silly gypsy bitch in a caravan, you can buy for three pounds?

FRANK: No, of course not! –

SOPHIE [*with grandeur*]: I practise here in this hideous town an art as old, as sacred as medicine. Look at this! [*She shoots out her hand.*] This hand has held the hand of a Royal Duchess in intimate spiritual communion. It has held the hand of an Archimandrite – a Prince of the Orthodox Church, who said to me, *bowing* to me, 'Baroness, you are not just a fortune-teller: you have the divine gift!' All right, I have – what is it? – *'come down'* in the world! Come down to Grinmouth! Down to pizza stalls and grease in the air! Dodge-them cars and rifle guns and all the fun in the fairground! Every day now – if I see anybody at all! – my *noble* clients are people like old potatoes wearing paper hats saying 'Kiss Me!' Whispering old spinsters, smelling of camphor – old red men with gin in their eyes, begging me to predict just one football pool to make them rich for life! *Rubbish people,* all of them, *killing* me to death with their middle-class dreams! But one thing, mister – I may hate them, but I never cheat them. Lemberg never lies!

    [*A pause.* SOPHIE *glares at him:* FRANK *is mortified.*]

FRANK: I'm sorry.

SOPHIE: That's all right. Go now, please.

[FRANK *rises and goes out in silence through the curtain and into the ante-room.* SOPHIE *sits staring after him, clasping her hands together in anxiety.*]

SOPHIE [*sotto voce*]: Five pounds! Five pounds, five whole pounds...!

[*Suddenly,* FRANK *returns, abruptly.*]

FRANK: Look, I really am sorry! It was disgusting to do that. I'm sorry: I see that now ... But I'm desperate, Baroness. I love this girl. I'd do anything to keep her. Tom is ruthless. You can't understand that. Someone from your world couldn't possibly understand ... I'm sorry. Good-bye. [*As abruptly, he makes to go again.*]

SOPHIE [*stopping him*]: One moment, please! [*A slight pause.*] I misjudged you, mister, I thought you were like him. The two of you were together in my mind. I thought: tummy-twisters! Head-bobbers! No sensitivity or gentleness about them. But I was wrong ... [*She rises.*] I see after all you have a faithful nature. I have come to believe that faithfulness in love is like real music – one of the marvels of the past. It is good to find it still exists. Look, there he is: coming back!

[*We hear the sound of* TOM's *whistling. He strolls into view on the upper level of the pier: in his hand is a large, woolly toy dog.* SOPHIE *and* FRANK *watch him through the window, as he stands looking at the sea, making slight dance movements with an air of confident conceit.*] Look at him. Ja: I see it now. Tummy-twister ... Taker! ... What you said: the *arrogance*! ... You're kind about him, because you are a kind man. 'Disarming', you call him. Well, mister, he doesn't disarm me! I see what he is. I see them every day, the new savages! I watch them on this pier, whistling up and down with their stupid fuzzy hair, stumbling along in their stupid high shoes, sequins on their shoulders, pretending to be amusing and eccentric – but really, underneath, just thugs! Working-class thugs! They think they own the world. Ja, and we let them think it. *We* – you and I – the foolish ones, the romantics, the *square* ones as they see us. Well, for once one of *them* is going to get it! A taker gets it from a giver! . . . [*Briskly*] I'll help you, mister! I'll keep your girl safe for you. I'll frighten the sequins right off this monster of yours! Give me the envelope.

[SOPHIE *stretches out her hand for the envelope.* TOM *turns to the stairs.* FRANK *hesitates.*]

Quick, quick, quick, quick!

[FRANK *hands it over.*]

It will cost you ten pounds.

FRANK: Ten?!

SOPHIE: Of course, ten. Do you think I compromise my art for nothing? Take it or leave it.

FRANK: All right.

[TOM *comes down the stairs.*]

SOPHIE: Good, then! Sssssh, he's coming. Sit! Sit . . .!

[FRANK *sits at the table. So does she.*]

Now tell me quick, what colour is your girl?

FRANK: Blonde.

SOPHIE: More.

FRANK: She often wears a pink scarf round her head. She's very fond of that. A pink scarf. You can see it in there – [*pointing to the crystal ball*] – if you like.

SOPHIE: Ssssh!

[*They freeze as* TOM *enters the ante-room.*]

[*Raising her voice*] And you, my dear, your dominant colour is green – your lucky day of the week is Wednesday, and, as I said before, everything in your cards indicates activity, activity and again activity! That will be two pounds, please.

[FRANK *hands her ten pounds, very reluctantly. She counts them carefully.*]

SOPHIE: It's going to be a very busy year, believe me. Lemberg never lies.

FRANK: Well, thank you, Baroness.

SOPHIE: Thank you. I wonder if your friend has returned.

FRANK [*raising his voice*]: Tom!

TOM: Yeh.

SOPHIE: Ah: good. Ask him to be kind enough to wait one minute, please. [*Indicating the envelope*] I'll call when I'm ready.

FRANK: Of course. Good-bye now.

SOPHIE: Good-bye.

FRANK [*for* TOM's *benefit, at the curtain*]: And thank you again.

[FRANK *goes through into the ante-room. Hastily,* SOPHIE *sits at the table. tears open the envelope and starts reading it.*]

[*To* TOM]: Hallo.

TOM: Well, how is she?

[*This ensuing scene is sotto voce.*]

FRANK: She's – she's all right . . .

TOM: What did she tell you?

FRANK: Nothing, actually . . . Actually, she's lousy.

TOM: What d'you mean?

SOPHIE [*calling out*]: One moment, mister, please! I'll be with you immediately! [*Reading the notes*] 'Born nineteen fifty-three . . .' [*She writes it on her fan.*]

TOM: Is she really hopeless?

FRANK: Well, they're all fakes, aren't they?

TOM: Of course they're not!

FRANK: Well, this one didn't get a thing right! If you ask me, they should cancel her Witch licence.

TOM [*alarmed*]: Sssh!

FRANK: Why?

TOM: You mustn't call them that!

SOPHIE [*reading the notes: concentrating*]: 'Mining village – father drunkard.' [*She writes on her fan.*]

FRANK [*seeing the toy dog*]: What the hell's that?

TOM: I won it. There's a rifle stall by the turnstiles. They were so glad to see me, they virtually gave it to me. I'll give it Sue.

FRANK: He looks drunk to me.

TOM: It's all that fresh air. It's knocked the poor bugger out!

SOPHIE [*to the photograph, whispering*]: Why are you staring at me? It's ten pounds, that's all that matters ... And anyway, surely, it is a major duty of the aristocracy to give lessons when necessary. [*She turns the photograph away from her and takes another drink, knocking it back.*]

TOM: What's she doing in there? Is she in a trance or something?

FRANK: I don't know. I think she calls it preparing.

TOM: You mean like meditation. It probably is.

FRANK: I bet she's just taking a quick zizz, poor old cow!

TOM [*furious*]: Ssssh! I *told* you!

SOPHIE [*reading the notes*]: 'Boxing Day – ran away from home – Boxing Day.' [*She writes it on her fan.*]

FRANK [*in sudden panic*]: Look – why don't you just come back with me?

TOM: What for?

FRANK: Because it really is a waste of money. This *one* is!

TOM [*slyly*]: Here – there's nothing funny about her, is there? Are you sure she didn't tell you something?

FRANK: Nothing, not a damn thing!

TOM: Well, you look a bit funny to me.

FRANK: I'm bored, that's all. I'm just plain bored! You'll hate it!

SOPHIE [*reading*]: 'Pink scarf ...'

TOM: Well, I'm here now, and she's seen me, so I might as well go in.

FRANK: Tom, listen to me!

SOPHIE [*calling out*]: I'm ready, mister. Enter, please! [*Reading the last note again, and putting away the envelope*] 'Pink scarf – *pink scarf* ...'

TOM [*to FRANK*]: I'll see you back there.

FRANK: All right. Don't say I didn't warn you ...

TOM [*'setting' the stuffed dog on him*]: Arf! Arf! Arf! ... You just go and check that system.

[TOM *chucks the dog on a chair, and lounges into the parlour.* FRANK *lingers for a second.*]

SOPHIE: Come in, mister. Sit down ...

[TOM *stays by the curtain – turns and lifts it, to find* FRANK *still there.*]

TOM [*coldly, to* FRANK]: Did I eavesdrop on *you?*

[FRANK *leaves in confusion. He goes up the iron stairs and off out of sight.* TOM *lets the curtain fall, and approaches the table where* SOPHIE *sits waiting.*]

SOPHIE: So. Here is my scale of charges. [*She hands him a card.*] Two pounds for cards alone. Two pounds fifty, cards and palms. Three pounds for the crystal ball. I recommend the ball. It is more profound.

TOM [*agreeing*]: Yeh.

SOPHIE: You're an addict, I think.

TOM: Addict? You mean drugs?

SOPHIE: Divination. You go often to consult people.

TOM [*surprised*]: That's right. actually. Does it show?

SOPHIE: You have comparing eyes.

TOM: Oh. That's no fun, is it?

SOPHIE [*coldly*]: They don't disturb me, mister. When you are older, you will learn that you can't go *shopping* in the world of the occult. People with the gift do not live in supermarkets, you know. Give me something you wear, please. Your scarf will do ...

[*Warily he hands her his scarf.*]

Thank you. Now please sit.

[*He sits.*]

And we begin. [*She takes the cover off the ball.*] There. Just a ball of glass. Except that nothing is *just* anything.

TOM: Of course not.

SOPHIE [*abruptly*]: Sssh! Don't speak, please. [*She puts his scarf on the ball.*] You are a musician.

[TOM *nods, surprised.*]

[*Sarcastically*] It's not such an amazing guess, mister. I've just finished reading your friend, after all. I hope he was satisfied.

TOM: Oh ... Yes ...

SOPHIE: He has good emanations. He is going to have a very happy domestic life.

TOM: Yeh?

SOPHIE [*hostile*]: Yeh. [*She stares at him. A pause.*] We begin now. What month were you born?

TOM: May.

SOPHIE: Taurus. Impetuous. Sometimes ruthless.

TOM.: Twenty-fifth

SOPHIE: Gemini. Interesting. [*She removes the handkerchief and peers savagely into the ball.*] It's very disturbed. Much confusion. Nineteen fifty-three. You were born in nineteen fifty-three.

TOM [*amazed*]: Yes!

SOPHIE: It's ritualistic, the ball. Often it gives first the date of birth, then the place. Ja, exactly. Now I see a house – a little narrow house in a dirty street. At the end a huge wheel turning in the sky. A coal-wheel! – a coal-village ... I see I'm not too far from the truth.

[*TOM can only nod, speechless. Covertly she consults her fan for more details, and goes on peering into the ball.*]

There is no woman in the house. Your mother is dead, ja? Your father, still alive. At least I see a man in working clothes. A bad face. Brutal face. Thick like a drunken man.

[*They exchange stares. TOM is very disturbed.*]

And now? I see a child. A little pale face. Eyes of fear, looking here – there – for escape. Such a frightened face. He ill-treated you, this father? He beat you?

[*TOM rises and begins to pace about.*]

What is this now? A fire. Something burning on it – it looks like a guitar ...

[*He turns on her, startled.*]

Can that be right, a guitar? What is that? Some symbol of your music talent?

TOM: No ...

SOPHIE: I disturb you, mister.

TOM: You see that?

SOPHIE: Very plain.

TOM: But you can't. You just *can't* – because it's here – my head. It's in here!...

SOPHIE: And for me it is *there*! Mister, you can lock nothing away. Time that happened once for you, happens *now* for me. Why did he do that, your father? To stop you being a musician? To hurt you?

[TOM *suddenly stops short, struck by something.*]

Maybe I should stop now?

TOM: No. Go on. What else do you see?

SOPHIE [*addressing herself again to the ball*]: You left home in the North, came to London.

TOM [*in a dead voice*]: Boxing Day. Lunch in Euston Station. Veal and ham pie!

SOPHIE: But you were fortunate in your friends. Recent time has been good for you. The ball is golden ... [*Peering harder*] But now ... [*Recoiling*] Oh!

TOM: What?

SOPHIE: Not any more. Not golden now. Going!

TOM: Can you see anything particular?

SOPHIE: Gold to grey. Dark. Now pink in dark. Hair. Pink hair – no, pink scarf – pink something, running, but into darkness ... You have a girl friend?

[*He shrugs, then nods.*]

She is in flight. I see her shadow, running in the dark. And after, another shadow: desire running, too. It's – *You*, I think! Running! running! one shadow trying to take the other! But now – another comes ... Oh, it's so confused.

TOM: Tell me!

SOPHIE: Ssssh! [*Peering fiercely*] This new shadow is much bigger. Ja: another man. It grows – swarms up over everything, you and her both – enormous red shadow up over everything! Over the grey, over the pink, over the dark, the red – the – red, the – red – *red* – RED!! [*She breaks off with a cry of distress.*]

TOM: What is it?

SOPHIE: No!

TOM: What?

SOPHIE [*in a tone of awe*]: I have seen it. *The blood-flash*! I have seen it.

TOM: The blood – ?

SOPHIE: Blood-flash. The most rare vision in divination. Red blood, drowning the ball. I have read about this, but never have I seen it till now, running over the glass ... It means – the most terrible warning.

TOM: Warning?

[*She rises impressively.*]

SOPHIE [*solemnly*]: You are doing something that is not good, mister. If you continue – disaster will strike at you. Disaster. And very soon. I mean it, mister. I'm sorry.

[*A pause.* TOM *lowers his head, as if he is crying.*]

If there is anything in your emotional life which is not what it should be – I beg of you: beware! If there is a girl in your life at the moment, she is not for you ...!

[*But she has to break off:* TOM *is not crying – he is laughing! She stares at him, scandalized. He laughs until he nearly chokes. Finally the noise subsides, with difficulty. She waits, outraged.*]

TOM: How much did he pay you?

SOPHIE: Pay?

TOM: Well, how did he set it up? He must have offered you a few quid on the side. He couldn't have expected you to do it for nothing.

SOPHIE: What do you mean, please?

TOM [*rising, wiping his eyes with his scarf*]: All the same, it's fantastic! I mean, what's the point? Is it supposed to be a joke? Fun and games by the sea?

SOPHIE: Mister, are you suggesting I've been bribed?

TOM: I'm not suggesting it. I'm saying it.

SOPHIE: How dare you? How absolutely bloody dare you?

TOM: Because I absolutely bloody know, that's how! There's only one person in the world I've ever told those things about my child-hood, and that's Frank.

SOPHIE [*loftily*]: My dear mister, to a professional eye like mine, truth does not have to be told. It is evident.

TOM: I dare say. And what if it *isn't* the truth?

[*A long pause.*]

SOPHIE: I beg your pardon?

TOM: What if it's a zonking great lie? Like every word of that story?

SOPHIE: I don't believe it.

TOM: It's true.

SOPHIE: Impossible. You say this to discredit me.

TOM: Why should I do that?

SOPHIE: Look, mister – what I see, I see. Lemberg never lies!

TOM: No, but *I do!*

[*Another pause.*]

SOPHIE [*carefully*]: You mean – your father is not a miner?

TOM: No. He's a rich accountant living in Leeds. [*He sits again, indolently.*]

SOPHIE: And your mother is not dead?

TOM: Not in the biological sense, no. She likes her game of golf, and gives bridge parties every Wednesday.

SOPHIE: But your accent!

TOM [*dropping it completely*]: I'm afraid that's as put on as everything else. I mean, there's no point changing your background if you're going to keep your accent, now is there?

SOPHIE [*astounded*]: Beloved God!

TOM: Actually, it slips a bit when I'm drunk, but people just think I'm being affected.

SOPHIE [*trying to grasp it*]: You mean to say – you live your whole life like this? One enormous great *lie* from morning to night?

TOM: Yes, I suppose I do.

SOPHIE: *Unimaginable!*

TOM: Does it worry you?

SOPHIE: Doesn't it worry you?

TOM: Not particularly. I regard it as a sort of . . .

SOPHIE: White lie?

TOM: Yes, very good! A white lie . . .

SOPHIE: But why? In heaven's name, why? Why? . . . WHY?

TOM: Well, it's a question of image, really. When I was a kid, in pop music you had to be working-class to get anywhere at all. Middle class was right out. Five years ago no one believed you can sing with the authentic voice of the people if you're the son of an accountant – and here we are!

SOPHIE: Incredible. And your parents, do they know that you have abolished them completely – like they never existed?

TOM: No, but it doesn't matter. They've abolished *me*, after all. How real am I to them? Dad calls me 'Minstrel Boy' whenever I go home, because he finds it embarrassing to have a singer for a son. And Mother tells her bridge club I'm in London studying music – because *studying* is a more respectable image for her than performing in a cellar. Both of them are talking about themselves, not me. And that's fine, because that's what everybody's doing all the time, everywhere. Do you dig?

SOPHIE: But at least you've told this girl friend? She knows the truth?

TOM: Sue? No.

SOPHIE: You mean you just go on and on telling her lies about your terrible childhood?

TOM: She likes it. She finds it all very sad.

SOPHIE: That's the most disgusting thing I ever heard! Do you think you can borrow suffering – just to make yourself attractive?

TOM: I know I can.

SOPHIE: He was right, your friend. You're a monster.

[TOM *turns. A pause.*]

TOM: Is that what he said?

SOPHIE: His word exact. A monster.

TOM [*laughing*]: I don't believe it.

SOPHIE: Of course not. All the same, to me it's obvious. I can see it now quite clearly.

TOM: As clearly as you saw my past life in that ball?

SOPHIE: Don't be impertinent. Remember, please, who you are speaking to. You are in the presence of a Baroness of the Holy Roman Empire!

[SOPHIE *glares at him, wrapping her shawl tighter about her. Bewildered, he gets up and goes into the ante-room.*]

SOPHIE [*calling out, very angry*]: There will be no charge!

TOM [*equally upset*]: Oh, thank you!

[*He stands shaking his head, trying to understand. Hastily* SOPHIE *rises and takes a swig from the decanter.*]

Monster? What?... I don't get any of this...

[*He returns unexpectedly. She takes the decanter hastily from her lips.*]

I don't understand! What's been going on?

SOPHIE [*trying to recover her dignity*]: Going on?

TOM: You tell me!

SOPHIE: Look, mister: it was a joke. Your friend is a joker. He made up this whole thing to amuse you. He said to me life was a bit grim for you at the moment. The engagement here was not so good – you were both down in the mouth. He suggested I cheered you up...!

TOM: No.

SOPHIE: I assure you.

TOM: That's not it.

SOPHIE: Of course it is. Most certainly: what else? Do you imagine I would do such a thing for real? Ja, ja, to amuse, why not? But *seriously* – to betray my art? *Do you think I would?*

TOM [*working it out*]: You had to see disaster for me and Sue. If we – she and me got together ... He's trying to warn me. Warn me off... My God! [*His mouth opens in amazement.*]

SOPHIE: So he's jealous. Is that so astounding ...? He's right to be, isn't he?

TOM: What d'you mean?

SOPHIE: Look, I know you, mister. I know you very well. Don't look at me like that – 'Oh my God!' 'What do you mean?' I'm

not ashamed of what I did! I took money under false pretences.
Good. Good, good, good – because for a good good purpose.

TOM: What are you talking about?

SOPHIE: Please go now. Absolutely at once! There's no point to
discuss further. There really isn't . . .

TOM [*alarmed*]: Just tell me this, first. How long has he known about
me and Sue?

[*She looks at him sharply.*]

Did he say? A couple of weeks? A month? I mean, Jesus, to be
that *hidden*! Not to give one sign. Just wait, day after day – build
up and build up – keep your face smiling all the time. And then
come down here for the day, pull a stunt like this – thinking about
it all the way down in the van, I suppose . . . I mean, *who is he*?

SOPHIE: A giver.

TOM: What?

SOPHIE: A giver, mister. Impossible for you to imagine, of course,
you taker. Someone who just gives, over and over to the end . . .
Hidden, you call him. Of course. Just because he's too proud to
show the pain he feels. He is now walking by the sea asking that
same question about you: '*Who is he*? What does he want? I gave
him everything. Admiration. Not enough! Security. Not enough!
I take him out of a slum – absolutely broke – give him my own
flat to share, not one penny in rent – not enough! I make him a
job. A whole group I form for him. White satin – engagements –
everything so he can fulfil his talent, not just sing for pennies in a
filthy pub.'

TOM: He told you *that*?

SOPHIE: Ja, mister, he told me. The poor idiot. He doesn't know
about people like you. Take and take and take until the cows are
at home. Take his hope, take his happiness – everything – everything you find!

TOM [*breaking*]: Here, I'm off!

SOPHIE: Ja, run! Run! The truth is unbearable, isn't it?

TOM: The what?

SOPHIE: The truth. *The truth*, mister! It's a meaningless word to you, isn't it?

[*A pause.* TOM *stands by the door, controlling himself.* SOPHIE *stands by the table, breathing heavily.*]

TOM [*quietly*]: All right. Just for the record, for the record, that's all – I'll give you three straight facts. Then I'll go . . . When I met him I wasn't broke. I wasn't living in a slum. And I'd formed my Group a good year before I set eyes on him.

SOPHIE: The White Liars.

TOM: That's right.

SOPHIE: Liars, yes – liars is right!

TOM [*protesting*]: We had a regular gig every Friday at the Iron Duke in the Commercial Road! You can check on that, if you like.

SOPHIE: Black liars! Black! Not white!

TOM [*insistently*]: He used to come every weekend with Sue, and sit in the corner listening to us. I just remember eyes – his brown ones and her big blue ones – and they'd sit there and groove on us for hours, just like they were the only people in the world who knew about us. Yeh – that's it! Like we were simply part of their private world, with no existence anywhere else . . .

[*He comes back into the room. She is suddenly listening.*]

Then suddenly one night, about six months ago, he comes over to me – says his name's Frank – he's a freelance journalist, and wants to do a whole story on the Liars for one of the Sunday papers. What they call a Study in Depth. It'll mean living around us for a while – did I mind? Well, it sounded great to me. I said fine. And there it was. I mean that's how it all began – with me chasing publicity! . . . A whole month – no, longer – he just followed us about, *observing*. Endless notes in a little book. Always grinning. Silly, you know, but very likeable. He was a mad talker: you couldn't stop him, for anything. I used to tell him, a journalist is supposed to listen, not yap all the time, but he'd just laugh. 'I like talking,' he'd say: 'It's the best thing in the world, after eating.' I was living out in Winchmore Hill then, with my Aunt Daisy.

Too much glazed chintz, but definitely not a slum. The only kind of music she likes is the sort you can chew tea-cakes to. In the end I left and moved in with him. I hadn't been there a week before I discovered he owed three months' rent.

SOPHIE: No!

TOM: Which I paid.

SOPHIE: I don't believe you.

TOM: And a week after that, I found out he wasn't really a journalist at all. He worked with Sue in a boutique in the King's Road.

SOPHIE: That's not true.

TOM: Till he was sacked.

SOPHIE: You're making it up.

TOM: Why should I do that? Look, can't you dig? ... From the moment Frank came in here he handed you a pack of lies. One after another.

[FRANK *returns, comes down the stairs and enters the ante-room.*]

SOPHIE: Fibs, maybe. That's possible.

TOM: Lies.

SOPHIE: Stories.

TOM: *Lies!* Zonking great *lies!*

SOPHIE [*suddenly furious*]: All right, lies, so what? *So what?* So he did, so he tells a couple of – of tales just to make himself a little more important – You dare! *You* dare talk about liars! You, with your coal-mines, guitar on the fire – your whole disgusting childhood!

TOM: *His!*

SOPHIE: What?

TOM: *His! His* lies! All of them.

SOPHIE: *His* lies? About *your* childhood?

TOM [*more softly*]: His and hers together. Theirs.

[*Gulls and wind are heard.* FRANK, *standing by the curtain in the ante-room, listens intently.*]

SOPHIE [*carefully*]: Mister, I don't know what the hell you are saying.

TOM: If I said they'd made me up, would you get it? If I said they'd made *me* make me up. That's nearer . . . I don't know. Sometimes I see it, just for a second, a bit of it. Then it clouds over, just like in your ball – and becomes a nightmare . . . [*He moves slowly to the crystal ball on the table.*] If only that thing really worked. If it could really show why. Why things happen.

SOPHIE: That's what it does, mister.

TOM: Yes, but to me. [*He picks the ball up.*] If I had the gift – just for five minutes to see the whole thing – her and him and me . . . How does it work? Colours, isn't it? Red for rage, black for death? What for fake? Brown? That's good. Butch brown: the sound of my accent: the phoney Yorkshire I put on when I came south, mainly because I couldn't stand my own voice. [*In a Yorkshire accent*] Butch brown! Colour of the moors . . .!

[FRANK *reacts, startled.* TOM *sits at the table, holding the ball.*]

[*Dropping the accent*] My grandpa used to talk like that, much to my mother's shame: I worked it up from him. It's what first turned them on: especially Frank. He used to sit on the end of my bed with his pencil and notebook, just grooving on it. Bogus journalist interviewing bogus miner! 'You're so lucky,' he'd say: 'so lucky to be born a prole. The working class is the last repository of instinct.' I'd just shrug, in my flannel pyjamas. Shrugs are perfect. You can imply anything with a good shrug: repository of instinct – childhood misery – whatever's wanted. [*He sets down the ball.*] What colour's that? The Want? The crazy Want in someone for an image to turn him on? Yeh – and the crazy way you play to it, just to make him feel good! Green, I bet you. Green for nausea . . . [*Simply*] I watched him make up my childhood. 'Where were you born?' he'd ask me. Then right away, he'd answer himself. 'Some godawful little cottage in the North, I suppose: no loo, I suppose, no electric light, I suppose.' 'I suppose' meaning 'I want'. And me, I'd shrug. Shrug, shrug: up goes his slum. Shrug, shrug: down comes Dad's belt: ow! Anything. I made bricks out of shrugs. Slagheaps. Flagellant fathers and blanketless winters, and stolen crusts gnawed in the outside lav! His eyes would pop. 'My

God, how we treat kids in this country!' Hers, too – Sue's: no, hers were worse. They'd brim with tears. She was the world's champion brimmer!... She cried the first night we ever...

[FRANK *gives a start; his hand flies up to his mouth; he strains to hear more.* TOM *rises and grows more urgent.*]

She had this flat on her own, right near the boutique. One night I'd been over for spaghetti, and I'd played a bit to her after. Suddenly – chord of E major still fading into the Chelsea drizzle – she's looking down at me, and her voice is all panty. 'You were *born* with that,' she says. 'There's the natural music of working people in your hands!' And down comes her hair – a curtain of buttermilk over my mouth. And there it is. The Want. I know it right away; the same Want as his, all desperate under her hair – 'Give it me. An image. Give me an image! Turn me on!'... What do you do? Buttermilk hair across your aching mouth, what do you do? Mouth opens – starts to speak – how can you stop it? [*In his Yorkshire accent*] 'You *understand*,' it says, dead sincere. 'Christ, you understand!... I'll tell you. The only encouragement my dad ever gave me was to throw my guitar on the fire. It wasn't much of an instrument, of course, but it was all I could afford...' [*Dropping the accent*] Oh green! Green for nausea! And blue, blue, blue for all the tears in her sky – dropping on me! Spattering me! Lashing the Swedish rug like rain on a Bank Holiday beach! I was soaked. I really was. I went to bed with her to get dry. Honest.

[*A slight pause.* TOM *starts to walk about the room. His voice betrays increasingly more desperation.* FRANK *stands rigid now. The light has faded considerably.*]

That was three months ago. When did he find out? *She* didn't tell him. She wouldn't dare... He guessed. Well, of *course* he guessed! They know each other completely. They *are* each other!... Yes.

[*A pause.* TOM *and* SOPHIE *look at each other.*]

Once I'd spoken – actually spoken a lie out loud – I was theirs. They got excited, like lions after meat, sniffing about me, drooling.

I suppose I could have stopped it any time. Just by using my own voice – telling them who I was. But I didn't. Colour the ball yellow. I told myself I didn't want to hurt them. But why not? Who was I? I didn't exist for them. I don't *now*! [*Excitedly*] They want *their* Tom: not me. Tom the idol. Tom the Turn-on. Tom the Yob God, born in a slum, standing in his long-suffering, mal-treated skin – all tangled hair and natural instinct – to be hung by his priests in white satin! . . . Yeh: that's the real colour for it all. *White*. Our uniform for the Liars. He designed it – she made it – I wear it! You should see me in it! Frothy white lace round the working-class throat! [*In his Yorkshire accent*] 'I look right hand-some in it!'

SOPHIE [*crying out*]: Stop it, now, mister! Stop it! Words on words on words on words. What *he* did – what *she* did – what *they* did! And all to escape the guilt of what *you* did!

TOM: I?

SOPHIE: Of course, you! *You* told the lies, didn't you? *You* needed the worship. The fact remains. Mr Taker, he gave you everything he had.

TOM: He gave me a role, that's what he gave! Can't you see that? I'm just acting in a film projected out of their eyes. 'I Was a Prisoner on Wet Dream Island!'

SOPHIE: Oh, ha, ha, ha. Very funny! The truth is much simpler than that, mister. Simpler and much more nasty.

TOM: Is it?

SOPHIE: A boring, familiar, nasty old story! You had a friend. He had a girl. You stole her. And that's all. [*Pause.*] Actually he has not guessed you have been sleeping with her three months. He just feared you might, one day soon . . . It's why he came here with his stupid game. Poor fellow. Poor stupid fellow . . . Ja, but people in love do many desperate things. You wouldn't under-stand that, of course. Good-bye, mister.

[*A pause.*]

TOM [*simply*]: Love, you really are in the wrong business, aren't you?

SOPHIE: What do you mean?

TOM: Excuse me.

[*TOM goes out suddenly into the ante-room.*]

SOPHIE [*calling after him*]: What do you mean, please?

[*TOM sees FRANK standing there, in the gloom. FRANK is very upset.*]

TOM: How long have you been there?

FRANK: Few minutes.

SOPHIE [*to herself*]: Beloved God! [*She stands rigidly, trying to listen.*]

TOM: You heard.

FRANK: No. No. Nothing ... Heard what? I – I – I've just this second come in ...

TOM: Good-bye, Frank.

[*TOM goes out of the ante-room and on to the pier.*]

FRANK: Where are you going? Tom!

[*FRANK follows TOM outside.*]

Where are you going?

TOM [*in a very posh accent*]: Back to Lichfield, old boy – back home.

FRANK: No! You can't ... All right, it was disgusting – it was a stupid bloody trick: I'm sorry. It was plain awful, I know – I know. But you just can't go like this. You can't just go!

TOM: What else would you suggest?

FRANK: Well, we could – we could – surely we ...

TOM: I've had it, Frank. With you. With her. With me, actually. You were right about one thing. The word you used. 'Monster.'

FRANK: I didn't mean that.

TOM: You should.

FRANK: That was the heat of the moment!

TOM: Tara, Frank. [*He puts out his hand.*]

FRANK: Tom, please. Can't we talk about this?

[*TOM shakes his head, smiles awkwardly, then suddenly turns and runs up the steps and out of sight.*]

[*Calling after him*] Tom! You've got the concert! [*Howling suddenly*] TOM!

[*He stands still. Gulls and wind. Then slowly he goes back inside.*]

SOPHIE *has seen* TOM *running away. Now she hears* FRANK *return and stand in the ante-room.*]

SOPHIE: Mister – Mister, won't you come in here, please?

[FRANK *stays where he is. She addresses him, unseen, from the darkening parlour.*]

I'm sorry. It's not gone so well, our little trick. It exploded, didn't it? I'm afraid that is sometimes the way with tricks ... Still, it's not so bad, is it? After all, it's what you wanted really – him to go away. 'Make him go,' you asked me. 'Get rid of him for me.' Well, I can't claim I did it myself, but it's been done, mister. He's gone. You won't see him again. It's not such a bad day's work, after all. Your girl is quite safe now: that's the important thing.

[*A faint sob comes from the ante-room.*]

Mister? ... Mister ...?

[*The sobs grow louder.* FRANK *is in agony.* SOPHIE *moves across the parlour to the ante-room, draws the curtain and enters it.* FRANK *turns away from her.*]

Oh come now, please. I don't understand.

FRANK: No, you don't, do you?

SOPHIE: You wanted him to go.

[*He turns on her.*]

FRANK: I wanted him to leave her alone! ... And to stay with me. In – my – bed.

[*She stares at him.*]

He'd been there six months.

[*A pause. Slowly* SOPHIE *retreats from the ante-room, back into the parlour. She stands by the curtain, deeply upset.*]

SOPHIE: He's right, your friend. I'm in the wrong business. I see nothing. I understand nothing, any more. I'm in the wrong place. The wrong world. *Who are you all?* You weird people – you young, weird, mad people! I was brought up in a proper world. People were clear, what they were – what they wanted! People were decent! I don't understand this world now – freaks and frauds and turn me on! I don't understand *anything anymore!* It's all so ugly! [*She grows more and more desperate.*] I was born into a world of order and beauty! That's what it meant to be noble – to give order to the world, and beautiful things. Not just tummy-twisting and wow-wow-wow like sick dogs! There was beauty, mister. My father brought me up in beauty, to respect beauty – to respect *people* – not make jokes of them – not dress like lunatics and make fun of people! I knew the Old World, mister! I knew the real world! My father, he knew the real world! He taught me how to live – my father; he taught me beauty – he taught me truth – he knew everything, my father – beauty and music and loving – he knew everything, everything – he knew NOTHING!

[*With a sudden swipe she smashes the photograph off the table on to the floor.* FRANK *is startled by the noise. She stares at the picture with hatred. Her speech gets more and more upset, but does not lose rapidity.*] Weak, stupid little man! Folded his hands in front of the world, and said nothing. Just nothing! Every day on the twenty-seven bus, for fourteen years. Eight forty-five leave the house, back at seven smelling of gherkins! Gherkins have a smell, mister – you know that smell? The smell of delicatessens? I said he was what to you? A Baron? Don't believe it. Take comfort, mister – here's a bit of comfort. It's not only the young who lie, whatever I said, it's not true – the old are worse. They are the biggest liars of them all! He was not a Baron; I am not a Baroness; my mother was not a Romany noblewoman, she was just a gypsy – and not even interesting. Just a quarter-gypsy, not colourful with scarves and lovers – just dull. Dull lady, always frightened. Both of them, always frightened! He had no estates, my dear: his estate was a Kosher delicatessen in the town of Innsbruck. After Hitler, he worked exactly at the same trade in London. Gherkins in Innsbruck, gherkins in Crawford Street – the Prater Deli: Proprietor Harry Plotkin. That is my real name: *Plotkin!* I started the fortune-telling because I could not bear to stand behind a counter and spoon out pickles! My mother said, 'It's beneath you to tell fortunes.' *Beneath!* Do you hear? Better of course to ladle out gherkins all your life into little cartons! 'Thank you, madame, that will be two pounds forty . . . Thank you, sir! Thank you, thank you!'

[FRANK *suddenly makes a move: he cannot bear any more. He starts for the door – suddenly he notices the toy dog. He picks it up.*]

The photograph you saw, that is a costume. [*She takes the crystal ball, recovers it and carries it back to its shelf.*] The Paddington Opera Society presented *The Count of Luxembourg*, and my father got into the chorus. I found the medals myself for him, in the Portobello Road. They are not exactly accurate.

[FRANK *walks slowly out of the door, and away up the stairs, holding the dog. He disappears into the evening.* SOPHIE *does not realize he has left. She kneels down and picks up the photograph. Her speech grows a little more tender but no slower.*]

One thing I told you was true. His clarinet. After he came here he never touched it: but in Austria he played quite well. And there *was* a lake. It wasn't ours, but we went there every year, two weeks in the summer, and stayed at a guest house on the shore. One year the Rosé Quartet was staying there also for a couple of nights, appearing at the Salzburg Festival. And one evening, for a quarter of an hour, they let him play with them: the slow movement of the Brahms. I sat on a chair on the grass. I watched him. He looked unbelievable. He narrowed his eyes behind his pince-nez, and he concentrated everything inside him, and he made no mistakes at all. Not one. They let him play the whole movement. And just as he finished the sun went down, just like that, went absolutely out like a light, exactly as if it had been arranged. And that was the best moment of his life . . . [*She gets up, and replaces the photograph. She is half crying.*] Well, well, well: other years, other tears . . .

[*The lights on the pier suddenly come on: a bright string of little bulbs. She raises her voice in the gloom, to the ante-room.*]

Why are you crying, mister? For *whom*? Your lover? What lover? There never *was* one! *Who did you lose, you stupid boy?* . . . You hear me, mister? You want my advice? Advice and Consultation! Go home now – go home and find someone *real*! That's my advice to you, mister – and it's good. It's the best. I tell you something: *Plotkin Never Lies!* Do you hear me, mister? That's my joke for today. *Plotkin Never Lies!* [*She pours herself a drink.*] That's my joke for tomorrow.

[*Gulls and wind.* SOPHIE *salutes the gulls with her glass, and drinks. The light fades on her, into darkness, as –*

THE CURTAIN FALLS

BLACK COMEDY

A FARCE IN ONE ACT

CHARACTERS

Black Comedy was first presented at Chichester by the National Theatre on 27 July 1965, and subsequently at the Old Vic Theatre, London, with the following cast:

BRINDSLEY MILLER	Derek Jacobi
CAROL MELKETT	Louise Purnell
MISS FURNIVAL	Doris Hare
COLONEL MELKETT	Graham Crowden
HAROLD GORRINGE	Albert Finney
SCHUPPANZIGH	Paul Curran
CLEA	Maggie Smith
GEORG BAMBERGER	Michael Byrne

BRINDSLEY MILLER: A young sculptor (mid-twenties), intelligent and attractive, but nervous and uncertain of himself.

CAROL MELKETT: His fiancée. A young debutante; very pretty, very spoiled; very silly. Her sound is that unmistakable, terrifying deb quack.

MISS FURNIVAL: A middle-aged lady. Prissy and refined. Clad in the blouse and sack skirt of her gentility, her hair in a bun, her voice in a bun, she reveals only the repressed gestures of the middle-class spinster – until alcohol undoes her.

COLONEL MELKETT: CAROL's commanding father. Brisk, barky, yet given to sudden vocal calms which suggest a deep and alarming instability. It is not only the constant darkness which gives him his look of wide-eyed suspicion.

HAROLD GORRINGE: The bachelor owner of an antique-china shop, and BRINDSLEY's neighbour, HAROLD comes from the North of England. His friendship is highly conditional and possessive: sooner or later, payment for it will be asked. A specialist in emotional blackmail, he can become hysterical when slighted, or (as inevitably happens) rejected. He is older than BRINDSLEY by several years.

SCHUPPANZIGH: A German refugee, chubby, cultivated, and effervescent. He is an entirely happy man, delighted to be in England, even if this means being employed full time by the London Electricity Board.

CLEA: BRINDSLEY's ex-mistress. Mid-twenties; dazzling, emotional, bright and mischievous. The challenge to her to create a dramatic situation out of the darkness is ultimately irresistible.

GEORG BAMBERGER: An elderly millionaire art collector, easily identifiable as such. Like the Electrician, he is a German.

THE SET: The action of the play takes place in BRINDSLEY's apartment in South Kensington, London. This forms the ground floor of a large house now divided into flats. HAROLD GORRINGE lives opposite; MISS FURNIVAL lives above.

There are four ways out of the room. A door at the left, upstage, leads directly across the passage to HAROLD's room. The door to this, with its mat laid tidily outside, can clearly be seen. A curtain, upstage centre, screens BRINDSLEY's studio: when it is parted we glimpse samples of his work in metal. To the right of this an open stair shoots steeply up to his bedroom above, reached through a door at the top. To the left, downstage, a trap in the floor leads down to the cellar.

It is a gay room, when we finally see it, full of colour and space and new shapes. It is littered with marvellous objects – mobiles, mannikins, toys, and dotty bric-à-brac – the happy paraphernalia of a free and imaginative mind. The total effect is of chaos tidied in honour of an occasion, and of a temporary elegance created by the furniture borrowed from HAROLD GORRINGE and arranged to its best advantage.

This consists of three elegant Regency chairs in gold leaf; a Regency chaise-longue to match; a small Queen Anne table bearing a fine opaline lamp, with a silk shade; a Wedgwood bowl in black basalt; a good Coalport vase containing summer flowers; and a fine porcelain Buddha.

The only things which actually belong to BRINDSLEY are a cheap square table bearing the drinks; an equally cheap round table in the middle of the room, shrouded by a cloth and decorated with the Wedgwood bowl; a low stool downstage centre, improved by the Buddha; a record player; and his own artistic creations. These are largely assumed to be in the studio awaiting inspection; but one of them is visible in this room. On the dais stands a bizarre iron sculpture dominated by two long detachable metal prongs, and hung with metal pieces which jangle loudly if touched. On the wall hang paintings, some of them presumably by CLEA. All are non-figurative: colourful geometric designs, splashes, splodges and splats of colour; whirls and whorls and wiggles – all testifying more to a delight in handling paint than to an ability to achieve very much with it.

THE TIME: 9.30 on a Sunday night.

THE LIGHT: On the few occasions when a lighter is lit, matches are struck or a torch is put on, the light on stage merely gets dimmer. When these objects are extinguished, the stage immediately grows brighter.

BLACK COMEDY

[*Complete darkness. Two voices are heard:* BRINDSLEY *and* CAROL. *They must give the impression of two people walking round a room with absolute confidence, as if in the light. We hear sounds as of furniture being moved. A chair is dumped down.*]

BRINDSLEY: There! How do you think the room looks?

CAROL [*quacking*]: Fabulous! I wish you could always have it like this. That lamp looks divine there. And those chairs are just the right colour. I told you green would look well in here.

BRINDSLEY: Suppose Harold comes back?

CAROL: He is not coming back till tomorrow morning.

[BRINDSLEY *paces nervously.*]

BRINDSLEY: I know. But suppose he comes tonight? He's mad about his antiques. What do you think he'll say if he goes into his room and finds out we've stolen them?

CAROL: Don't dramatize. We haven't stolen *all* his furniture. Just three chairs, the sofa, that table, the lamp, the bowl, and the vase of flowers, that's all.

BRINDSLEY: And the Buddha. That's more valuable than anything. Look at it.

CAROL: Oh, do stop worrying, darling.

BRINDSLEY: Well, you don't know Harold. He won't even let anyone touch his antiques.

CAROL: Look, we'll put everything back as soon as Mr Bamberger leaves. Now stop being dreary.

BRINDSLEY: Well, frankly, I don't think we should have done it. I mean – *anyway*, Harold or no.

CAROL: Why not, for heaven's sake? The room looks divine now. Just look at it!

BRINDSLEY: Darling. Georg Bamberger's a multi-millionaire. He's lived all his life against this sort of furniture. Our few stolen bits aren't going to impress him. He's coming to see the work of an unknown sculptor. If you ask me, it would look much better to him if he found me exactly as I really am: a poor artist. It might touch his heart.

CAROL: It might – but it certainly won't impress Daddy. Remember, he's coming too.

BRINDSLEY: As if I could forget! Why you had to invite your monster father tonight, I can't think!

CAROL: Oh, not again!

BRINDSLEY; Well, it's too bloody much. If he's going to be persuaded I'm a fit husband for you, just by watching a famous collector buy some of my work, he doesn't deserve to have me as a son-in-law!

CAROL: He just wants some proof you can earn your own living.

BRINDSLEY: And what if Bamberger *doesn't* like my work?

CAROL: He will, darling. Just stop worrying.

BRINDSLEY: I can't. Get me a whisky.

[*She does. We hear her steps, and a glass clink against a bottle – then the sound of a soda syphon.*]

I've got a foreboding. It's all going to be a disaster. An A1, copper-bottomed, twenty-four-carat disaster!

CAROL: Look, darling, you know what they say. Faint heart never won fair ladypegs!

BRINDSLEY: How true.

CAROL: The trouble with you is you're what Daddy calls a Determined Defeatist.

BRINDSLEY: The more I hear about your Daddy, the more I hate him. I loathe military men anyway . . . and in any case, he's bound to hate me.

CAROL: Why?

BRINDSLEY: Because I'm a complete physical coward. He'll smell it on my breath.

CAROL: Look, darling, all you've got to do is stand up to him. Daddy's only a bully when he thinks people are afraid of him.

BRINDSLEY: Well, I am.

CAROL: You haven't even met him.

BRINDSLEY: That doesn't make any difference.

CAROL: Don't be ridiculous. [*Hands him a drink*] Here.

BRINDSLEY: Thanks.

CAROL: What can he do to you?

BRINDSLEY: For one thing, he can refuse to let me marry you.

CAROL: Ah, that's sweetipegs!

[*They embrace.*]

BRINDSLEY: I like you in yellow. It brings out your hair.

CAROL: Straighten your tie. You look sloppy.

BRINDLSEY: Well, you look divine.

CAROL: Really?

BRINDSLEY: I mean it. I've never seen you look so lovely.

CAROL: Tell me, Brin, have there been many before me?

BRINDSLEY: Thousands.

CAROL: Seriously!

BRINDSLEY: Seriously – none.

CAROL: What about that girl in the photo?

BRINDSLEY: She lasted about three months.

CAROL: When?

BRINDSLEY: Two years ago.

CAROL: What was her name?

BRINDSLEY: Clea.

CAROL: What was she like?

BRINDSLEY: She was a painter. Very honest. Very clever. And just about as cosy as a steel razor-blade.

CAROL: When was the last time you saw her?

BRINDSLEY [*evasively*]: I told you . . . two years ago.

145

CAROL: Well, why did you still have her photo in your bedroom drawer?

BRINDSLEY: It was just there. That's all. Give me a kiss ... [*Pause.*] No one in the world kisses like you.

CAROL [*murmuring*]: Tell me something ... did you like it better with her – or me?

BRINDSLEY: Like what?

CAROL: Sexipegs.

BRINDSLEY: Look, people will be here in a minute. Put a record on. It had better be something for your father. What does he like?

CAROL [*crossing to the record player*]: He doesn't like anything except military marches.

BRINDSLEY: I might have guessed ... Wait – I think I've got some! That last record on the shelf. The orange cover. It's called 'Marching and Murdering with Sousa', or something.

CAROL: This one?

BRINDSLEY: That's it.

CAROL [*getting it*]: 'The Band of the Coldstream Guards.'

BRINDSLEY: Ideal. Put it on.

CAROL: How'd you switch on?

BRINDSLEY: The last knob on the left. That's it ... Let us pray! ... Oh God, let this evening go all right! Let Mr Bamberger like my sculpture and buy some! Let Carol's monster father like me! And let my neighbour Harold Gorringe never find out that we borrowed his precious furniture behind his back! Amen.

[*A Sousa march; loud. Hardly has it begun, however, when it runs down – as if there is a failure of electricity. The sound stops.*

Brilliant light floods the stage. The rest of the play, save for the times when matches are struck, or for the scene with SCHUPPANZIGH, *is acted in this light, but as if in pitch darkness.*

They freeze: CAROL *by the end of the sofa;* BRINDSLEY *by the drinks table. The girl's dress is a silk flag of chic wrapped round her greyhound's body. The boy's look is equally cool: narrow, contained and sexy. Throughout the evening, as things slide into disaster for*

146

him, his crisp, detached shape degenerates progressively into sweat and rumple – just as the elegance of his room gives way relentlessly to its usual near-slum appearance. For the place, as for its owner, the evening is a progress through disintegration.]

God! We've blown a fuse!

[*The structure and appearance of* BRINDSLEY's *room is described in the note at the beginning of the play.*]

CAROL: *Oh no!*

BRINDSLEY: It must be. [*He blunders to the light switch, feeling ahead of him, trying to part the darkness with his hands. Finding the switch, he flicks it on and off.*]

CAROL: It is!

BRINDSLEY: Oh no!

CAROL: Or a power cut. Where's the box?

BRINDSLEY: In the hall.

CAROL: Have you any candles?

BRINDSLEY: No. Damn!

CAROL: Where are the matches?

BRINDSLEY: They should be on the drinks table. [*Feeling round the bottles*] No. Try on the record player.

[*They both start groping about the room, feeling for matches.*]

Damn, damn, damn, damn, damn, damn!

[CAROL *sets a maracca rattling off the record player.*]

CAROL: There! [*Finding it*] No . . .

[*The telephone rings.*]

BRINDSLEY: Would you believe it! [*He blunders his way towards the sound of the bell. Just in time he remembers the central table – and stops himself colliding into it with a smile of self-congratulation.*] All right: I'm coming! [*Instead he trips over the dais, and goes sprawling – knocking the phone onto the floor. He has to grope for it on his knees, hauling the receiver back to him by the wire. Into receiver.*] Hallo? . . . [*In sudden horror*] Hallo! . . . No, no, no, no – I'm fine, just fine! . . . You? . . . [*His hand over the receiver: to* CAROL] Darling – look in the bedroom, will you?

CAROL: I haven't finished in here yet.

BRINDSLEY: Well, I've just remembered there's some fuse wire in the bedroom. In that drawer where you found the photograph. Go and get it, will you?

CAROL: I don't think there is. I didn't see any there.

BRINDSLEY [*snapping*]: Don't argue. Just look!

CAROL: All right. Keep your hairpiece on!

[*During the following she gropes her way cautiously up the stairs – head down, arms up the banisters, silken bottom thrust out with the effort.*]

BRINDSLEY [*controlling himself*]: I'm sorry. I just know it's there, that's all. You must have missed it.

CAROL: What about the matches?

BRINDSLEY: We'll have to mend it in the dark, that's all. Please hurry, dear.

CAROL [*climbing*]: Oh God, how dreary!

BRINDSLEY [*taking his hand off the receiver and listening to hear* CAROL *go*]: Hallo? ... Well, well, well, well! How are you? Good. That's just fine. Fine, fine! ... Stop saying what?

[CAROL *reaches the top of the stairs – and from force of habit pulls down her skirt before groping her way into the bedroom.*]

BRINDSLEY [*hand still over the receiver*]: Carol? ... Darling? ... [*Satisfied she has gone; in a rush into the telephone, his voice low*] Clea! What are you doing here? I thought you were in Finland ... But you've hardly been gone six weeks ... Where are you speaking from? ... The air terminal? ... Well, no, that's not a good idea tonight. I'm terribly busy, and I'm afraid I just can't get out of it. It's business.

CAROL [*calling from the bedroom door, above*]: There's nothing there except your dreary socks. I told you.

BRINDSLEY [*calling back*]: Well, try the other drawers! ... [*He rises as he speaks, turning so that the wire wraps itself around his legs.*]

[CAROL *returns to her search.*]

[*Low and rapid, into phone*] Look: I can't talk now. Can I call you tomorrow? Where will you be? ... Look, I told you *no*, Clea. Not tonight. I know it's just around the corner, that's not the point! You can't come round ... Look, the situation's changed. Something's happened this past month –

CAROL [*off*]: I can't see anything. Brin, *please!* –

BRINDSLEY: Clea, I've got to go ... Look, I can't discuss it over the phone ... Has it got to do with what? Yes, of course it has. I mean you can't expect things to stay frozen, can you?

CAROL [*emerging from the bedroom*]: There's nothing here. Haven't we any matches at all?

BRINDSLEY: Oh stop wailing! [*Into phone*] No, not you. I'll call you tomorrow. Good-bye. [*He hangs up sharply – but fails to find the rest of the telephone so that he bangs the receiver hard on the table first. Then he has to disentangle himself from the wire. Already* BRINDSLEY *is beginning to be fussed.*]

CAROL [*descending*]: Who was that?

BRINDSLEY: Just a chum. Did you find the wire?

CAROL: I can't find anything in this. We've *got* to get some matches! –

BRINDSLEY: I'll try the pub. Perhaps they'll have some candles as well.

[*Little screams are heard approaching from above. It is* MISS FURNIVAL *groping her way down in a panic.*]

MISS FURNIVAL [*squealing*]: Help! Help! ... Oh please someone help me!

BRINDSLEY [*calling out*]: Is that you, Miss Furnival?

MISS FURNIVAL: Mr Miller? ...

BRINDSLEY: Yes?

MISS FURNIVAL: Mr Miller!

BRINDSLEY: Yes!

[*She gropes her way in.* BRINDSLEY *crosses to find her, but narrowly misses her.*]

MISS FURNIVAL: Oh, thank God, you're there; I'm so frightened!

BRINDSLEY: Why? Have your lights gone too?

MISS FURNIVAL: Yes!

BRINDSLEY: It must be a power cut.

[*He finds her hand and leads her to the chair downstage left.*]

MISS FURNIVAL: I don't think so. The street lights are on in the front. I saw them from the landing.

BRINDSLEY: Then it must be the main switch of the house.

CAROL: Where is that?

[MISS FURNIVAL *gasps at the strange voice.*]

BRINDSLEY: It's in the cellar. It's all sealed up. No one's allowed to touch it but the electricity people.

CAROL: What are we going to do?

BRINDSLEY: Get them – quick!

CAROL: Will they come at this time of night?

BRINDSLEY: They've got to.

[BRINDSLEY *accidentally touches* MISS FURNIVAL's *breasts. She gives a little scream.* BRINDSLEY *gropes his way to the phone.*]

Have you by any chance got a match on you, Miss Furnival?

MISS FURNIVAL: I'm afraid I haven't. So improvident of me. And I'm absolutely terrified of the dark!

BRINDSLEY: Darling, this is Miss Furnival, from upstairs. Miss Furnival – Miss Melkett.

MISS FURNIVAL: How do you do?

CAROL [*extending her hand into the darkness*]: How do you do?

MISS FURNIVAL: Isn't this frightful?

[BRINDSLEY *picks up the phone and dials 'O'.*]

CAROL: Perhaps we can put Mr Bamberger off.

BRINDSLEY: Impossible. He's dining out and coming on here after. He can't be reached.

CAROL: Oh, flip!

BRINDSLEY [*sitting on the dais, and speaking into the phone*]: Hallo, Operator, can you give me the London Electricity Board, please? Night Service . . . I'm sure it's in the book, Miss, but I'm afraid I can't see . . . There's no need to apologize. No, I'm not blind – I just can't see! We've got a fuse . . . No we *haven't* got any matches!

[*Desperate*] Miss, *please*: this is an emergency! . . . Thank you! . . . [*To the room*] London is staffed with imbeciles!

MISS FURNIVAL: Oh, you're so right, Mr Miller.

BRINDSLEY [*rising, frantic: into the phone*]: Miss, I *don't want* the number: I can't dial it! . . . Well, have *you* ever tried to dial a number in the dark? . . . [*Trying to keep control*] I just want to be connected . . . Thank you. [*To* MISS FURNIVAL] Miss Furnival, do you by any remote chance have any candles?

MISS FURNIVAL: I'm afraid not, Mr Miller.

BRINDSLEY [*mouthing nastily at her*]: 'I'm afraid not, Mr Miller' . . . [*Briskly, into phone*] Hallo? Look, I'd like to report a main fuse at 18 Scarlatti Gardens. My name is Miller. [*Exasperated*] Yes, yes! All right . . . ! [*Maddened: to the room*] Hold on! Hold bloody on! . . .

MISS FURNIVAL: If I might suggest – Harold Gorringe opposite might have some candles. He's away for the weekend, but always leaves his key under the mat.

BRINDSLEY: What a good idea. That's just the sort of practical thing he would have. [*To* CAROL] Here – take this . . . I'll go and see, love. [*He hands her the telephone in a fumble – then makes for the door – only to collide smartly with his sculpture.*] Bugger!

MISS FURNIVAL: Are you all right, Mr Miller?

BRINDSLEY: I knew it! I bloody knew it. This is going to be the worst night of my life! . . . [*He collides with the door.*]

CAROL: Don't panic, darling. Just don't panic!

[*He stumbles out and is seen groping under* HAROLD'*s mat for the key. He finds it and enters the room opposite.*]

MISS FURNIVAL: You're so right, Miss Melkett. We must none of us panic.

CAROL [*on the phone*]: Hallo? Hallo? [*To* MISS FURNIVAL] This would have to happen tonight. It's just Brindsley's luck.

MISS FURNIVAL: Is it something special tonight then, Miss Melkett?

CAROL: It couldn't be more special if it tried.

MISS FURNIVAL: Oh, dear. May I ask why?

CAROL: Have you ever heard of a German called Georg Bamberger?

MISS FURNIVAL: Indeed, yes. Isn't he the richest man in the world?

CAROL: Yes. [*Into phone*] Hallo? . . . [*To* MISS FURNIVAL] Well, he's coming here tonight.

MISS FURNIVAL: Tonight!

CAROL: In about twenty minutes, to be exact. And to make matters worse, he's apparently stone deaf.

MISS FURNIVAL: How extraordinary! May I ask why he's coming?

CAROL: He saw some photos of Brindsley's work and apparently got madly excited about it. His secretary rang up last week and asked if he could come and see it. He's a great collector. Brin would be absolutely *made* if Bamberger bought a piece of his.

MISS FURNIVAL: Oh, how exciting!

CAROL: It's his big break. Or was – till a moment ago.

MISS FURNIVAL: Oh, my dear, you *must* get some help. Jiggle that thing.

CAROL [*jiggling the phone*]: Hallo? Hallo? . . . Perhaps the Bomb's fallen, and everyone's dead.

MISS FURNIVAL: Oh, please don't say things like that – even in levity.

CAROL [*someone answers her at last*]: Hallo? Ah! This is Number 18, Scarlatti Gardens. I'm afraid we've had the most dreary fuse. It's what's laughingly known as the Main Switch. We want a *little man*! . . . Well, they can't *all* have flu . . . Oh, please try! It's screamingly urgent . . . Thank you. [*She hangs up.*] Sometime this evening, they hope. That's a lot of help.

MISS FURNIVAL: They're not here to help, my dear. In my young days you paid your rates and you got satisfaction. Nowadays you just get some foreigner swearing at you. And if they think you're of the middle class, that only makes it worse.

CAROL: Would you like a drink?

MISS FURNIVAL: I don't drink, thank you. My dear father, being a Baptist minister, strongly disapproved of alcohol.

[*A scuffle is heard amongst milk bottles off, followed by a stifled oath.*]

COLONEL MELKETT [*off*]: Damn and blast!! . . . [*Barking*] Is there anybody there?

CAROL [*calling*]: In here, daddypegs!

COLONEL: Can't you put the light on, dammit? I've almost knocked meself out on a damn milk bottle.

CAROL: We've got a fuse. Nothing's working.

[COLONEL MELKETT *appears, holding a lighter which evidently is working – we can see the flame, and, of course, the lights go down a little.*]

MISS FURNIVAL: Oh what a relief! A light!

CAROL: This is my father, Colonel Melkett, Miss Furnival. She's from upstairs.

COLONEL: Good evening.

MISS FURNIVAL: I'm taking refuge for a moment with Mr Miller. I'm not very good in the dark.

COLONEL: When did this happen?

[MISS FURNIVAL, *glad for the light, follows it pathetically as the* COLONEL *crosses the room.*]

CAROL: Five minutes ago. The main just blew.

COLONEL: And where's this young man of yours?

CAROL: In the flat opposite. He's trying to find candles.

COLONEL: You mean he hasn't got any?

CAROL: No. We can't even find the matches.

COLONEL: I see. No organization. Bad sign!

CAROL: Daddy, please. It could happen to any of us.

COLONEL: Not to me.

[*He turns to find* MISS FURNIVAL *right behind him and glares at her balefully. The poor woman retreats to the sofa and sits down.*]

[COLONEL MELKETT *gets his first sight of* BRINDSLEY'S *sculpture.*] What the hell's that?

CAROL: Some of Brindsley's work.

COLONEL: Is it, by Jove? And how much does that cost?

CAROL: I think he's asking fifty pounds for it.

COLONEL: My God!

CAROL [*nervously*]: Do you like the flat, Daddy? He's furnished it very well, hasn't he? I mean it's rich, but not gaudipegs.

COLONEL: Very elegant – good: I can see he's got excellent taste.

[*Seeing the Buddha*] Now that's what I understand by a real work of art – you can see what it's meant to be.

MISS FURNIVAL: Good heavens!

CAROL: What is it?

MISS FURNIVAL: Nothing ... It's just that Buddha – it so closely resembles the one Harold Gorringe has.

[CAROL *looks panic-stricken.*]

COLONEL: It must have cost a pretty penny, what? He must be quite well off ... By Jove – it's got pretty colours. [*He bends to examine it.*]

CAROL [*sotto voce, urgently, to* MISS FURNIVAL]: You *know* Mr Gorringe?

MISS FURNIVAL: Oh, very well indeed! We're excellent friends. He has such lovely things ... [*For the first time she notices the sofa on which she is sitting*] Oh ...

CAROL: What?

MISS FURNIVAL: This furniture ... [*Looking about her*] Surely – ? – my goodness! –

CAROL [*hastily*]: Daddy, why don't you look in there? It's Brin's studio. There's something I particularly want you to see before he comes back.

COLONEL: What!

CAROL: It – it – er – it's a surprise, go and see.

COLONEL: Very well, Dumpling. Anythin' to oblige. [*To* MISS FURNIVAL] Excuse me.

[*He goes off into the studio, taking his lighter with him. The light instantly gets brighter on stage.* CAROL *sits beside the spinster on the sofa, crouching like a conspirator.*]

CAROL [*low and urgent*]: Miss Furnival, you're a sport, aren't you?

MISS FURNIVAL: I don't know. What is this furniture doing in here? It belongs to Harold Gorringe.

CAROL: I know. We've done something absolutely frightful. We've stolen all his best pieces and put Brin's horrid old bits into *his* room.

MISS FURNIVAL: But why? It's disgraceful!

CAROL [*sentimentally*]: Because Brindsley's got nothing, Miss Furnival. Nothing at all. He's as poor as a church mouse. If Daddy had seen this place as it looks normally, he'd have forbidden our marriage on the spot. Mr Gorringe wasn't there to ask – so we just took the chance.

MISS FURNIVAL: If Harold Gorringe knew that anyone had touched his furniture or his porcelain, he'd go out of his mind! And as for that Buddha – [*pointing in the wrong direction*] – it's the most precious piece he owns. It's worth hundreds of pounds.

CAROL: Oh, please, Miss Furnival – you won't give us away, will you? We're desperate! And it's only for an hour ... Oh, please! *please!*

MISS FURNIVAL [*giggling*]: Very well! ... I won't betray you!

CAROL: Oh, thank you!

MISS FURNIVAL: But it'll have to go back exactly as it was, just as soon as Mr Bamberger and your father leave.

CAROL: I swear! Oh, Miss Furnival, you're an angel! Do have a drink. Oh, no, you don't. Well, have a bitter lemon.

MISS FURNIVAL: Thank you. That I won't refuse.

[*The* COLONEL *returns, still holding his lighter. The stage darkens a little.*]

COLONEL: Well, they're certainly a surprise. And that's supposed to be sculpture?

CAROL: It's not supposed to be. It is.

COLONEL: They'd make good garden implements. I'd like 'em for turnin' the soil.

[MISS FURNIVAL *giggles.*]

CAROL: That's not very funny, Daddy.

[MISS FURNIVAL *stops giggling.*]

COLONEL: Sorry, Dumpling. Speak as you find.

CAROL: I wish you wouldn't call me Dumpling.

COLONEL: Well, there's no point wastin' this. We may need it!

[*He snaps off his lighter.* MISS FURNIVAL *gives her little gasp as the stage brightens.*]

CAROL: Don't be nervous, Miss Furnival. Brin will be here in a minute with the candles.

MISS FURNIVAL: Then I'll leave, of course. I don't want to be in your way.

CAROL: You're not at all. [*Hearing him*] Brin? –

[BRINDSLEY *comes out of* HAROLD's *room – returns the key under the mat.*]

BRINDSLEY: Hallo?

CAROL: Did you find anything?

BRINDSLEY [*coming in*]: You can't find anything in this! If there's candles there, *I* don't know where they are. Did you get the electric people?

CAROL: They said they might send someone around later.

BRINDSLEY: How much later?

CAROL: They don't know.

BRINDSLEY: That's a lot of help. What a look-out! Not a bloody candle in the house. A deaf millionaire to show sculpture to – and your monster father to keep happy. Lovely!

COLONEL [*grimly lighting his lighter*]: Good evenin'.

[BRINDSLEY *jumps.*]

CAROL: Brin, this *is* my father – Colonel Melkett.

BRINDSLEY [*wildly embarrassed*]: Well, well, well, well, well! ... [*Panic*] Good evening, sir. Fancy you being there all the time! I – I'm expecting some dreadful neighbours, some neighbour monsters, monster neighbours, you know ... They rang up and said they might look round ... Well, well, well! ...

COLONEL [*darkly*]: Well, well.

MISS FURNIVAL [*nervously*]: Well, well!

CAROL [*brightly*]: Well!

[*The* COLONEL *rises and advances on* BRINDSLEY *who retreats before him across the room.*]

COLONEL: You seem to be in a spot of trouble.

BRINDSLEY [*with mad nervousness*]: Oh, not really! Just a fuse – nothing really, we have them all the time ... I mean, it won't be the first fuse I've survived, and I dare say it won't be the last! [*He gives a wild braying laugh.*]

COLONEL [*relentless*]: In the meantime, you've got no matches. Right?

BRINDSLEY: Right.

COLONEL: No candles. Right?

BRINDSLEY: Right.

COLONEL: No basic efficiency, right?

BRINDSLEY: I wouldn't say that, exactly . . .

COLONEL: By basic efficiency, young man, I mean the simple state of being At Attention in life, rather than At Ease. Understand?

BRINDSLEY: Well, I'm certainly not at ease.

COLONEL: What are you goin' to do about it?

BRINDSLEY: Do?

COLONEL: Don't echo me, sir. I don't like it.

BRINDSLEY: You don't like it . . . I'm sorry.

COLONEL: Now look you here. This is an emergency. Anyone can see that.

BRINDSLEY: No one can see anything: that's the emergency! [*He gives his braying laugh again.*]

COLONEL: Spare me your humour, sir, if you don't mind. Let's look at the situation objectively. Right?

BRINDSLEY: Right.

COLONEL: Good. [*He snaps off the lighter.*] Problem: Darkness. Solution: Light.

BRINDSLEY: Oh very good, sir.

COLONEL: Weapons: Matches: none! Candles: none! What remains?

BRINDSLEY: Search me.

COLONEL [*triumphantly*]: Torches. Torches, sir! what?

BRINDSLEY: Or a set of early Christians.

COLONEL: What did you say?

BRINDSLEY: I'm sorry. I think I'm becoming unhinged. Very good. Torches – brilliant.

COLONEL: Routine. Well, where would you find one?

BRINDSLEY: The pub. What time is it?

[*The* COLONEL *lights his lighter, but now not at the first try. The stage light flickers up and down accordingly.*]

COLONEL: Blasted thing. It's beginnin' to go. [*He consults his watch.*] Quarter to ten. You can just make it, if you hurry.

BRINDSLEY: Thank you, sir. Your clarity of mind has saved the day!

COLONEL: Well, get on with it, man.

BRINDSLEY: Yes, sir! Back in a minute!

[*The* COLONEL *sits in the Regency chair, downstage right.*]

CAROL: Good luck, darling.

BRINDSLEY: Thank you, my sweet.

[*She blows him a kiss. He blows her one back.*]

COLONEL [*irritated*]: Stop that at once!

[BRINDSLEY *starts for the door – but as he reaches it,* HAROLD GORRINGE *is heard, off.*]

HAROLD [*broad Lancashire accent*]: Hallo? Hallo? Anyone there?

BRINDSLEY [*freezing with horror*]: HAROLD!!

HAROLD: Brindsley?

BRINDSLEY [*meant for* CAROL]: It's Harold! He's back!

CAROL: Oh no!

BRINDSLEY: THE FURNITURE!!

HAROLD: What's going on here?

[HAROLD *appears. He wears a smart raincoat and carries a weekend suitcase. His hair falls over his brow in a flossy attempt at elegance.*]

BRINDSLEY: Nothing, Harold. Don't go in there – come in here. We've had a fuse. It's dark – it's all over the house.

HAROLD: Have you phoned the electric? [*Reaching out.*]

BRINDSLEY [*reaching out and grabbing him*]: Yes. Come in here.

HAROLD [*grabbed*]: Ohh! . . . [*He takes* BRINDSLEY'S *hand and enters the room cosily on his arm.*] It's rather cosy in the dark, isn't it?

BRINDSLEY [*desperately*]: Yes! I suppose so . . . So you're back from your weekend then . . .

HAROLD: I certainly am, dear. Weekend! Some weekend! It rained the whole bloody time. I feel damp to my knickers.

BRINDSLEY [*nervously*]: Well, have a drink and tell us all about it.

HAROLD: Us? [*Disengaging himself*] Who's here, then?

MISS FURNIVAL [*archly*]: I am, Mr Gorringe.

HAROLD: Ferny?

MISS FURNIVAL: Taking refuge, I'm afraid. You know how I hate the dark.

COLONEL [*attempting to light his lighter*]: Blasted thing! . . . [*He succeeds.*] There we are! [*Raising it to* GORRINGE's *face, with distaste*] Who are you?

BRINDSLEY: May I present my neighbour. This is Harold Gorringe – Colonel Melkett.

HAROLD: How do?

COLONEL: How d'ye do?

BRINDSLEY: And this is Miss Carol Melkett, Harold Gorringe.

CAROL [*giving him a chilly smile*]: Hallo! . . .

[HAROLD *nods coldly.*]

BRINDSLEY: Here, let me take your raincoat, Harold.

[*He is wearing a tight, modish, grey suit and a brilliant strawberry shirt.*]

HAROLD [*taking it off and handing it to him*]: Be careful, it's sopping wet.

[*Adroitly,* BRINDSLEY *drops the coat over the Wedgwood bowl on the table.*]

COLONEL: You got no candles, I suppose?

HAROLD: Would you believe it, Colonel, but I haven't! Silly me!

[BRINDSLEY *crosses and blows out the* COLONEL's *lighter, just as* HAROLD *begins to look round the room. The stage brightens.*]

COLONEL: What the devil did you do that for?

BRINDSLEY: I'm saving your wick, Colonel. You may need it later and it's failing fast.

[*The* COLONEL *gives him a suspicious look.* BRINDSLEY *moves quickly back, takes up the coat and drops it over the right end of the sofa, to conceal as much of it as possible.*]

HAROLD: It's all right. I've got some matches.

CAROL [*alarmed*]: Matches!

HAROLD: Here we are! I hope I've got the right end. [*He strikes one.*]

[BRINDSLEY *immediately blows it out from behind, then moves swiftly to hide the Wedgwood bowl under the table and drop the tablecloth over the remaining end of the sofa.* MISS FURNIVAL *sits serenely unknowing between the two covers.*]

Hey, what was that?

BRINDSLEY [*babbling*]: A draught. No match stays alight in this room. It's impossible. Cross currents, you know! Old houses are full of them. They're almost a permanent feature in *this* house . . .

HAROLD [*bewildered*]: I don't know what you're on about. [*He strikes another match.*]

[BRINDSLEY *again blows it out as he nips over to sit in the chair downstage left, but this time is seen.*]

HAROLD: What's up with you?

BRINDSLEY: Nothing!

HAROLD: Have you got a dead body in here or something?

BRINDSLEY: NO! [*He starts his maniacal laughter.*]

HAROLD: Here, have you been drinking?

BRINDSLEY: No. Of course not.

[HAROLD *strikes another match.* BRINDSLEY *dashes up. All these strikings and blowings are of course accompanied by swift and violent alterations of the light.*]

HAROLD [*exasperated*]: Now look here! What's up with you?

BRINDSLEY [*inspired*]: Dangerous!

HAROLD: What?

BRINDSLEY [*frantically improvising*]: Dangerous! It's dangerous! . . . We can all die! Naked flames! Hideous accidents can happen with naked flames!

HAROLD: I don't know what you're on about – what's up with you?

[BRINDSLEY *clutches* HAROLD *and backs him bewilderedly across to the centre table.*]

BRINDSLEY: I've just remembered! It's something they always warn you about. In old houses the fuse-box and the gas meter are in the same cupboard. They are here!

COLONEL: So what about it?

BRINDSLEY: Well . . . electrical blowouts can damage the gas supply. They're famous for it! They do it all the time! And they say you've got to avoid naked flames till they're mended.

COLONEL [*suspicious*]: I've never heard of that.

HAROLD: Me neither.

BRINDSLEY: Well, take my word for it. It's fantastically dangerous to burn a naked flame in this room!

CAROL [*catching on*]: Brin's absolutely right. In fact, they warned me about it on the phone this evening when I called them. They said, 'Whatever you do, don't strike a match till the fuse is mended.'

BRINDSLEY: There, you see! – it's terribly dangerous.

COLONEL [*grimly*]: Then why didn't you warn me, Dumpling?

CAROL: I – I forgot.

COLONEL: Brilliant!

MISS FURNIVAL: Oh goodness, we must take care!

BRINDSLEY: We certainly must! . . . [*Pause.*] Let's all have a drink. Cheer us up! . . .

CAROL: Good idea! Mr Gorringe, would you like a drink?

HAROLD: Well, I must say, that wouldn't come amiss. Not after the journey I've had tonight. I swear to God there was thirty-five people in that compartment if there was one – babes in arms, toddlers, two nuns, three yapping poodles, and not a sausage to eat from Leamington to London. It's a bloody disgrace.

MISS FURNIVAL: You'd think they'd put on a restaurant car, Mr Gorringe.

HAROLD: Not them, Ferny. They don't care if you perish once they've got your fare. Excuse me. I'll just go and clean up.

BRINDSLEY [*panic*]: You can do that here!

HAROLD: Well, I must unpack anyway.

BRINDSLEY: Do it later.

HAROLD: No, I hate to keep clothes in a suitcase longer than I absolutely have to. If there's one thing I can't stand, it's a creased suit.

BRINDSLEY: Five more minutes won't hurt, surely?

HAROLD: Ooh, you aren't half bossy!

CAROL: What will you have? Winnie, Vera or Ginette?

HAROLD: Come again?

CAROL: Winnie Whisky, Vera Vodka, or dear old standby Ginette.

HAROLD [*yielding*]: I can see you're the camp one! ... If it's all the same to you, I'll have a drop of Ginette, please, and a little lime juice.

COLONEL [*irritated*]: Young man, do I have to keep reminding you that you are in an emergency? You have a guest arrivin' any second.

BRINDSLEY: Oh God, I'd forgotten!

COLONEL: Try the pub. Try the neighbours. Try who you damn well please, sir – but *get a torch!*

BRINDSLEY: Yes ... Yes! ... Carol, can I have a word with you, please?

CAROL: I'm here.

[*She gropes towards him and* BRINDSLEY *leads her to the stairs.*]

COLONEL: What now?

BRINDSLEY: Excuse us just a moment, please, Colonel.

[*He pulls her quickly after him, up the stairs.*]

MISS FURNIVAL [*as they do this*]: Oh, Mr Gorringe, it's so exciting. You'll never guess who's coming here tonight.

HAROLD: Who?

MISS FURNIVAL: Guess.

HAROLD: The Queen!

MISS FURNIVAL: Oh, Mr Gorringe, you are ridiculous!

[BRINDSLEY *arrives at the top of the stairs, then opens the bedroom door and closes it behind them.*]

BRINDSLEY: What are we going to do?

CAROL [*behind the door*]: I don't know!

BRINDSLEY [*behind the door*]: Think!

CAROL: But –

BRINDSLEY: *Think!*

COLONEL: Is that boy touched or somethin'?

HAROLD: Touched? He's an absolute poppet.

COLONAL: A what?

HAROLD: A duck. I've known him for years, ever since he came here. There's not many secrets we keep from each other, I can tell you.

COLONEL [*frostily*]: Really?

HAROLD: Yes, really. He's a very sweet boy.

[BRINDSLEY *and* CAROL *emerge from behind the bedroom door.*]

BRINDSLEY: We'll have to put all Harold's furniture back in his room.

CAROL: *Now?!*

BRINDSLEY: We'll have to! I can't get a torch till we do.

CAROL: We can't!

BRINDSLEY: We must. He'll go *mad* if he finds out what we've done.

HAROLD: Well, come on, Ferny: don't be a tease. Who is it? Who's coming?

MISS FURNIVAL: I'll give you a clue. It's someone with money.

HAROLD: Money? . . . Let me think.

COLONEL [*calling out*]: Carol!

CAROL: Look, can't you just tell him it was a joke?

BRINDSLEY: You don't know him. He can't bear anyone to touch his treasures. They're like children to him. He cleans everything twice a day with a special swansdown duster. He'd wreck everything. Would you like him to call me a thief in front of your father?

CAROL: Of course not!

BRINDSLEY: Well, he would. He gets absolutely hysterical. I've seen him.

COLONEL [*mildly*]: Brindsley!

CAROL: Well, how the hell can we do it?

HAROLD: It's no good. You can't hear up there.

BRINDSLEY [*stripping off his jacket*]: Look, you hold the fort. Serve them drinks. Just keep things going. Leave it all to me. I'll try and put everything back in the dark.

CAROL: It won't work.

BRINDSLEY: It's *got* to!

COLONEL [*roaring*]: Brindsley!!

BRINDSLEY [*dashing to the door*]: Coming, sir ... [*With false calm*] I'm just getting some empties to take to the pub.

COLONEL: Say what you like. That boy's touched.

BRINDSLEY [*to* CAROL, *intimately*]: Trust me, darling.

[*They kiss.*]

COLONEL: At the double, Miller.

BRINDSLEY: Yes, sir! Yes, sir! [*He rushes out and in his anxiety he misses his footing and falls neatly down the entire flight of stairs. Picking himself up.*] I'm off now, Colonel! Help is definitely on the way.

COLONEL: Well, hurry it up, man.

BRINDSLEY: Carol will give you drinks. If Mr Bamberger arrives, just explain the situation to him.

HAROLD [*feeling for his hand*]: Would you like me to come with you?

BRINDSLEY: No, no, no – good heavens: stay and enjoy yourself!

[HAROLD *kisses his hand.* BRINDSLEY *pulls it away.*]

I mean, you must be exhausted after all those poodles. A nice gin and lime will do wonders. I shan't be a minute. [*He reaches the door, opens it, then slams it loudly, remaining on the inside. Stealthily he opens it again, stands dead still for a moment, centre, silently indicating to himself the position of the chairs he has to move – then he finds his way to the first of the Regency chairs, downstage left, which he lifts noiselessly.*]

CAROL [*with bright desperation*]: Well now, drinks! What's everyone going to have? It's Ginette for Mr Gorringe and I suppose Winnie for Daddy.

COLONEL: And how on earth are you going to do that in the dark?

CAROL: I remember the exact way I put out the bottles.

[BRINDSLEY *bumps into her with the chair and falls back, gored by its leg.*]

CAROL: It's very simple.

HAROLD: Oh look, luv, let me strike a match. I'm sure it's not that dangerous, just for a *minute*! [*He strikes a match.*]

CAROL: Oh no!...

> [BRINDSLEY *ducks down, chair in hand, and Carol blows out the match.*]

Do you want to blow us all up, Mr Gorringe? ... All poor Mr Bamberger would find would be teensy weensy bits of us. Very messypegs!

> [*She snatches the box of matches, feels for the ice bucket, and drops them into it.* BRINDSLEY *steals out, Felix-the-cat-like, with the chair as* CAROL *fumblingly starts to mix drinks. He sets it down, opens* HAROLD's *door, and disappears inside it with the chair.*]

HAROLD: Bamberger? Is that who's coming? Georg Bamberger?

MISS FURNIVAL: Yes. To see Mr Miller's work. Isn't it exciting?

HAROLD: Well, I never! I read an article about him last week in the Sunday paper He's known as the mystery millionaire. He's almost completely deaf – deaf as a post – and spends most of his time indoors alone with his collection. He hardly ever goes out, except to a gallery or a private studio. That's the life! If I had money that's what I'd do. Just collect all the china and porcelain I wanted.

> [BRINDSLEY *returns with a poor, broken-down chair of his own and sets it down in the same position as the one he has taken out. The second chair presents a harder challenge. It sits right across the room, upstage right. Delicately he moves towards it – but he has difficulty finding it. We watch him walk round and round it in desperately narrowing circles till he touches it and with relief picks it up.*]

MISS FURNIVAL: I've never met a millionaire. I've always wondered if they feel different to us. I mean their actual skins.

COLONEL: Their skins?

MISS FURNIVAL: Yes. I've always imagined they must be softer than ours. Like the skins of ladies when I was a girl.

CAROL: What an interesting idea.

HAROLD: Oh, she's very fanciful is Ferny. Real imagination, I always say.

MISS FURNIVAL: Very kind of you, Mr Gorringe. You're always so generous with your compliments.

[*As she speaks her next speech staring smugly into the darkness, hands clasped in maidenly gentility, the second Regency chair is being moved slowly across what should be her field of vision, two inches from her face. During the following,* BRINDSLEY *unfortunately mis-aims and carries the chair past the door, bumps into the wall, retreats from it, and inadvertently shuts the door softly with his back. Now he cannot get out of the room. He has to set down the chair, grope for the door handle, turn it, then open the door – then re-find the chair which he has quite lost. This takes a long and frantic time. At last he triumphs, and staggers from the room, nearly exhausted.*]

But this is by no means fancy. In my day, softness of skin was quite the sign of refinement. Nowadays, of course, it's hard enough for us middle classes to keep ourselves decently clothed, let alone soft. My father used to say, even before the bombs came and burnt our dear little house at Wendover: 'The game's up, my girl. We middle classes are as dead as the dodo.' Poor Father, how right he was.

[Note: *Hopefully, if the counterpoint of farce action goes well,* MISS FURNIVAL *may have to ad-lib a fair bit during all this, and not mind too much if nobody hears her. The essential thing for all four actors during the furniture-moving is to preserve the look of ordinary conversation.*]

COLONEL: Your father was a professional man?

MISS FURNIVAL: He was a man of God, Colonel.

COLONEL: Oh.

[BRINDSLEY *returns with a broken-down rocking-chair of his own. He crosses gingerly to where the* COLONEL *is sitting.*]

How are those drinks coming, Dumpling?

CAROL: Fine, Daddy. They'll be one minute.

COLONEL [*speaking directly into* BRINDSLEY'*s face*]: Let me help you.

[BRINDSLEY *staggers back, startled.*]

CAROL: You can take this bitter lemon to Miss Furnival if you want.

[BRINDSLEY *sets down the rocker immediately next to the* COLONEL'*s chair.*]

COLONEL: Very well.

[*He rises just as* BRINDSLEY's *hand pulls it from beneath him. With his other hand* BRINDSLEY *pulls the rocker into the identical position. The* COLONEL *moves slowly across the room, arms outstretched for the bitter lemon. Unknowingly* BRINDSLEY *follows him, carrying the third chair. The* COLONEL *collides gently with the table. At the same moment* BRINDSLEY *reaches it upstage of him, and searches for the Wedgwood bowl. Their hands narrowly miss. Then the* YOUNG MAN *remembers the bowl is under the table. Deftly he reaches down and retrieves it – and carrying it in one hand and the chair in the other, triumphantly leaves the room through the arch unconsciously provided by the outstretched arms of* CAROL *and the* COLONEL, *giving and receiving a glass of Scotch – which they think is lemonade.*]

CAROL: Here you are, Daddy. Bitter lemon for Miss Furnival.

COLONEL: Right you are, Dumpling. [*To* MISS FURNIVAL] So your father was a minister, then?

MISS FURNIVAL: He was a saint, Colonel. I'm only thankful he never lived to see the rudeness and vulgarity of life today.

[*The* COLONEL *sets off to find her but goes much too far to the right.*]

HAROLD [*he sits on the sofa beside her*]: Oooh, you're so right, Ferny. Rudeness and vulgarity – that's it to a T. The manners of some people today are beyond belief. Honestly. Did I tell you what happened in my shop last Friday? I don't think I did.

MISS FURNIVAL: No, Mr Gorringe, I don't think so.

[*Her voice corrects the* COLONEL's *direction. During the following he moves slowly up toward her.*]

HAROLD: Well, I'd just opened up – it was about quarter to ten and I was dusting off the teapots – you know, Rockingham collects the dust something shocking! – when who should walk in but that Mrs Levitt, you know – the ginger-haired bit I told you about, the one who thinks she's God's gift to bachelors.

COLONEL [*finding her head with his hand and presenting her with the Scotch*]: Here's your lemonade.

MISS FURNIVAL: Oh, thank you. Most kind.

[*Throughout* HAROLD's *story,* MISS FURNIVAL *nurses the glass, not drinking. The* COLONEL *finds his way slowly back to the chair he thinks he was sitting on before, but which is now a rocker.* BRINDSLEY *re-appears triumphantly carrying one of the original Regency chairs he took out. He moves slowly across the room getting his bearings.*]

HAROLD: Anyway, she's got in her hand a vase I'd sold her last week – it was a birthday present for an old geezer she's having a bit of a ding dong with somewhere in Earls Court, hoping to collect all his lolly when he dies, as I read the situation. I'm a pretty good judge of character, Ferny, as you know – and she's a real grasper if ever I saw one.

[*The* COLONEL *sits heavily in the rocking-chair which overbalances backward, spilling him onto the floor.*]

COLONEL: Dammit to hell!

CAROL: What's the matter, Daddy?

[*A pause.* BRINDSLEY *sits down panic-stricken on the chair he has carried in. The* COLONEL *feels the chair and sets it on its feet.*]

COLONEL [*unbelieving*]: It's a blasted rockin'-chair! I didn't see a blasted rockin'-chair here before! . . .

[*Astounded, the* COLONEL *remains on the floor.* BRINDSLEY *rises and moves the chair to the original position of the second chair he moved.*]

HAROLD: Oh yes, you want to watch that. It's in a pretty ropey condition. I've told Brin about it several times. Anyway, this vase. It's a nice bit of Kang Tsi, blue and white with a good orange-peel glaze, absolutely authentic – I'd let her have it for twenty-five pounds, and she'd got infinitely the best of the bargain, no arguments about that! –

[HAROLD *rises and leans against the centre table to tell his story more effectively. The* COLONEL *seats himself again, gingerly.*]

Well, in she prances, her hair all done up in one of them bouffon hair-dos, you know, tarty – French-like – it would have looked fancy on a girl half her age with twice her looks –

[BRINDSLEY *mistakenly lifts the end of the sofa.* MISS FURNIVAL *gives a little scream at the jolt.*]

HAROLD: Exactly! You know the sort.

[BRINDSLEY *staggers in the opposite direction downstage onto the* *rostrum.*]

And d'you know what she says to me? 'Mr Gorringe,' she says, 'I've been cheated.'

MISS FURNIVAL: No!

HAROLD: Her very words. 'Cheated.'

[BRINDSLEY *collides with the sculpture on the dais. It jangles viol-* *ently.*]

[*To it*] Hush up, I'm talking!

CAROL [*covering up*]: I'm frightfully sorry.

[HAROLD *whirls round, surprised.*]

HAROLD: Anyway – 'Oh, I say, and how exactly has that occurred, Mrs Levitt?' 'Well,' she says, 'quite by chance I took this vase over to Bill Everett in the Portobello, and he says it's not what you called it at all, Chinese and very rare. He says it's a piece of nineteenth-century English trash!'

[BRINDSLEY *finds the lamp on the downstage table and picks it up.* *He walks with it round the rocking-chair, on which the* COLONEL *is* *now sitting again.*]

'Does he?' I say. 'Does he?' I keep calm. I always do when I'm riled. 'Yes,' she says. 'He does. And I'd thank you to give me my money back!'

[*The wire of the lamp has followed* BRINDSLEY *round the bottom of* *the rocking-chair. It catches.* BRINDSLEY *tugs it gently. The chair* *moves. Surprised, the* COLONEL *jerks forward.* BRINDSLEY *tugs it* *again, much harder. The rocking-chair is pulled forwards, spilling the* COLONEL *out of it, again onto the floor, and then falling itself on* *top of him. The shade of the lamp comes off. During the ensuing* *dialogue* BRINDSLEY *gets to his knees and crawls right across the* *room following the flex of the lamp. He finds the plug, pulls it out,* *and – still on his knees – re-traces his steps, winding up the wire* *around his arm, and becoming helplessly entangled in it. The* COLONEL *remains on the floor, now really alarmed.*]

MISS FURNIVAL: How dreadful, Mr Gorringe. What did you do?

HAROLD: I counted to ten, and then I let her have it. 'In the first place,' I said, 'I don't expect my customers to go checking up on my honesty behind my back. In the second, Bill Everett is ignorant as Barnsley dirt, he doesn't know Tang from Ting. And in the third place, that applies to you, too, Mrs Levitt.'

MISS FURNIVAL: You didn't!

HAROLD: I certainly did – and worse than that. 'You've got in your hand,' I said, 'a minor masterpiece of Chinese pottery. But in point of fact,' I said, 'you're not even fit to hold a 1953 Coronation mug. Don't you ever come in here again,' I said, '– don't you cross my threshold. Because, if you do, Mrs Levitt, I won't make myself responsible for the consequences.'

CAROL [*with two drinks in her hand*]: My, Mr Gorringe, how splendid of you. Here's your gin and lime. You deserve it. [*She hands him the bitter lemon.*]

HAROLD [*accepting it*]: Ta. I was proper blazing, I didn't care.

CAROL: Where are you? Where are you, Daddy? Here's your Scotch.

COLONEL: Here, Dumpling!

[*He gets up dazedly and fumbles his way to the glass of gin and lime.* BRINDSLEY *meanwhile realizes he has lost the shade of the lamp. On his knees, he begins to look for it.*]

HAROLD: Carrotty old bitch – telling *me* about pottery! *Oooh!!* [*He shakes himself indignantly at the recollection of it.*]

MISS FURNIVAL: Do you care for porcelain yourself, Colonel?

COLONEL: I'm afraid I don't know very much about it, madam. I like some of that Chinese stuff – you get some lovely colours, like on that statue I saw when I came in here – very delicate.

HAROLD: What statue's that, Colonel?

COLONEL: The one on the packing case, sir. Very fine.

HAROLD: I didn't know Brin had any Chinese stuff. What's it of then, this statue?

[BRINDSLEY *freezes.*]

CAROL [*desperately*]: Well, we've all got drinks, I'd like to propose

Daddy's regimental toast. Raise your glasses everyone! 'To the dear old Twenty-fifth Horse. Up the British, and Death to the Enemy'!

MISS FURNIVAL: I'll drink to that! Up the British!

HAROLD: Up the old Twenty-fifth!!

[*Quickly* BRINDSLEY *finds the Buddha, moves it from the packing case to the table, then gets* HAROLD's *raincoat from the sofa, and wraps the statue up in it, leaving it on the table.*]

COLONEL: Thank you, Dumpling. That was very touchin' of you. Very touchin' indeed. [*He swallows his drink.*] Dammit, that's gin!

HAROLD: I've got lemonade!

MISS FURNIVAL: Oh! Horrible! . . . Quite horrible! That would be alcohol, I suppose! . . . Oh dear, how unpleasant! . . .

HAROLD [*to* MISS FURNIVAL]: Here, luv, exchange with me. No – you get the lemonade – but I get the gin. Colonel –

COLONEL: Here, sir.

[*Seizing her chance* MISS FURNIVAL *downs a huge draft of Scotch. They all exchange drinks.* BRINDSLEY *resumes his frantic search for the shade.*]

HAROLD: Here, Ferny.

[*The* COLONEL *hands her the gin and lime. He gets instead the bitter lemon from* HAROLD. HAROLD *gets the Scotch.*]

MISS FURNIVAL: Thank you.

HAROLD: Well, let's try again. Bottoms up!

COLONEL: Quite.

[*They drink. Triumphantly,* BRINDSLEY *finds the shade. Unfortunately at the same moment the* COLONEL *spits out his lemonade in a fury all over him, as he marches towards him on his knees.*]

Look here – I can't stand another minute of this! [*He fishes his lighter out of his pocket and angrily tries to light it.*]

CAROL: Daddy, please!

COLONEL: I don't care, Dumpling. If I blow us up, then I'll blow us up! This is *ridiculous*! . . .

[*His words die in the flame. He spies* BRINDSLEY *kneeling at his feet, wound about with lampwire.*]

What the devil are you doin' there?

BRINDSLEY [*blowing out his lighter*]: Now don't be rash, Colonel! Isn't the first rule of an officer 'Don't involve your men in unnecessary danger'? [*Quickly he steals, still on his knees, to the table downstage right.*]

COLONEL: Don't be impertinent. Where's the torch?

BRINDSLEY: Er . . . the pub was closed.

HAROLD: You didn't go to the pub in that time, surely? You couldn't have done.

BRINDSLEY: Of course I did.

MISS FURNIVAL: But it's five streets away, Mr Miller.

BRINDSLEY: Needs must when the Devil drives, Miss Furnival. Whatever that means. [*Quickly he lifts the table, and steals out of the room with it and the wrecked lamp.*]

COLONEL [*who thinks he is still kneeling at his feet*]: Now look here: there's somethin' very peculiar goin' on in this room. I may not know about art, Miller, but I know men. I know a liar in the light, and I know one in the dark.

CAROL: Daddy!

COLONEL: I don't want to doubt your word, sir. All the same, I'd like your oath you went out to that public house. *Well?*

CAROL [*realizing he isn't there, raising her voice*]: Brin, Daddy's talking to you!

COLONEL: What are you shoutin' for?

BRINDSLEY [*rushing back from* HAROLD'*s room, still entangled in the lamp*]: Of course! I know! He's absolutely right. I was – just thinking it over for a moment.

COLONEL: Well? What's your answer?

BRINDSLEY: I . . . I couldn't agree with you more, sir.

COLONEL: What?

BRINDSLEY: That was a very perceptive remark you made there. Not everyone would have thought of that. Individual. You know. Almost witty. Well, it *was* witty. Why be ungenerous? . . .

COLONEL: Look, young man, are you trying to be funny?

BRINDSLEY [*ingratiatingly*]: Well, I'll try anything once ...

HAROLD: I say, this is becoming a bit unpleasant, isn't it?

CAROL: It's becoming drearypegs.

COLONEL: Quiet, Dumpling. Let me handle this.

BRINDSLEY: What's there to handle, sir?

COLONEL: If you think I'm going to let my daughter marry a born liar, you're very much mistaken.

HAROLD: Marry!

CAROL: Well, that's the idea.

HAROLD: You and this young lady, Brin?

CAROL: Are what's laughingly known as engaged. Subject of course to Daddy's approval.

HAROLD: Well! [*Furious at the news, and at the fact that* BRINDSLEY *hasn't confided in him*] What a surprise! ...

BRINDSLEY: We were keeping it a secret.

HAROLD: Evidently. How long's this been going on, then?

BRINDSLEY: A few months.

HAROLD: You old slyboots.

BRINDSLEY [*nervous*]: I hope you approve, Harold.

HAROLD: Well, I must say, you know how to keep things to yourself.

BRINDSLEY [*placatingly*]: I meant to tell you, Harold ... I really did. You were the one person I was going to tell.

HAROLD: Well, why didn't you then?

BRINDSLEY: I don't know. I just never got around to it.

HAROLD: You saw me every day.

BRINDSLEY: I know.

HAROLD: You could have mentioned it at any time.

BRINDSLEY: I know.

HAROLD [*huffy*]: Well, it's your business. There's no obligation to share confidences. I've only been your neighbour for three years. I've always assumed there was more than a geographical closeness between us, but I was obviously mistaken.

BRINDSLEY: Oh, don't start getting huffy, Harold!

HAROLD: I'm not getting anything. I'm just saying it's surprising, that's all. Surprising and somewhat disappointing.

BRINDSLEY: Oh look, Harold, please understand –

HAROLD [*shrill*]: There's no need to say anything! It'll just teach me in future not to bank too much on friendship. It's silly me again! Silly, stupid, trusting me!

[MISS FURNIVAL *rises in agitation and gropes her way to the drinks table.*]

COLONEL: Good God!

CAROL [*wheedling*]: Oh come, Mr Gorringe. We haven't told anybody. Not one single soulipegs. Really.

COLONEL: At the moment, Dumpling, there's nothing to tell. And I'm not sure there's going to be!

BRINDSLEY: Look, sir, we seem to have got off on the wrong foot. If it's my fault, I apologize.

MISS FURNIVAL [*groping about on the drinks table*]: My father always used to say, 'To err is human: to forgive divine.'

CAROL: I thought that was somebody else.

MISS FURNIVAL [*blithely*]: So many people copied him. [*She finds the open bottle of gin, lifts it and sniffs it eagerly.*]

CAROL: May I help you, Miss Furnival?

MISS FURNIVAL: No, thank you, Miss Melkett. I'm just getting myself another bitter lemon. That is – if I may, Mr Miller?

BRINDSLEY: Of course. Help yourself.

MISS FURNIVAL: Thank you, most kind! [*She pours more gin into her glass and returns slowly to sit upstage on the edge of the rostrum.*]

COLONEL: Well, sir, wherever you are –

BRINDSLEY: Here, Colonel.

COLONEL: I'll overlook your damn peculiar behaviour this once, but understand this, Miller. My daughter's dear to me. You show me you can look after her, and I'll consider the whole thing most favourably. I can't say fairer than that, can I?

BRINDSLEY: No, sir. Most fair, sir. Most fair. [*He pulls a hideous face one inch from the* COLONEL'*s.*]

CAROL: Of course he can look after me, Daddy. His works are

going to be world-famous. In five years I'll feel just like Mrs Michelangelo.

HAROLD [*loftily*]: There wasn't a Mrs Michelangelo, actually.

CAROL [*irritated*]: Wasn't there?

HAROLD: No. *He* had passionate feelings of a rather different nature.

CAROL: Really, Mr Gorringe. I didn't know that. [*She puts out her tongue at him.*]

BRINDSLEY: Look, Harold, I'm sorry if I've hurt your feelings.

HAROLD [*loftily*]: You haven't.

BRINDSLEY: I know I have. Please forgive me.

CAROL: Oh, do, Mr Gorringe. Quarrelling is so dreary. I hope we're all going to be great friends.

HAROLD: I'm not sure that I can contemplate a friendly relationship with a viper.

MISS FURNIVAL: Remember: to err is human, to forgive divine!

COLONEL [*irritated*]: You just said that, madam.

[*CLEA enters, wearing dark glasses and carrying an air-bag. She stands in the doorway, amazed by the dark. She takes off her glasses, but this doesn't improve matters.*]

MISS FURNIVAL [*downing her gin happily*]: Did I?

CAROL: Brin's not really a viper. He's just artistic, aren't you, darling?

BRINDSLEY: Yes, darling.

[*CAROL sends him an audible kiss across the astonished CLEA. He returns it, equally audibly.*]

CAROL [*winningly*]: Come on, Mr Gorringe. It really is a case of forgive and forgettipegs.

HAROLD: Is it reallypegs?

CAROL: Have another Ginette and lime. I'll have one with you. [*She rises and mixes the drink.*]

HAROLD [*rising*]: Oh, all right. I don't mind if I do.

CAROL: Let me mix it for you.

HAROLD: Ta. [*He crosses to her, narrowly missing CLEA who is now crossing the room to the sofa, and gets his drink*] I must say there's nothing nicer than having a booze-up with a pretty girl.

CAROL [*archly*]: You haven't seen me yet.

HAROLD: Oh, I just know it. Brindsley always had wonderful taste. I've often said to him, you've got the same taste in ladies as I have in porcelain. Ta.

[HAROLD *and* BRINDSLEY – *one from upstage, one from across the room – begin to converge on the sofa. On the word 'modest' all three,* CLEA *in the middle, sit on it.* BRINDSLEY *of course imagines he is sitting next to* HAROLD.]

BRINDSLEY: Harold!

CAROL: Oh don't be silly, Brin. Why be so modest? I found a photograph of one of his bits from two years ago, and I must say she was pretty stunning in a blowsy sort of way.

HAROLD: Which one was that, then? I suppose she means Clea.

CAROL: Did you know her, Mr Gorringe?

HAROLD: Oh yes. She's been around a long time.

[BRINDSLEY *nudges* CLEA *warningly – imagining she is* HAROLD. CLEA *gently bumps* HAROLD.]

CAROL [*surprised*]: Has she?

HAROLD: Oh yes, dear. Or am I speaking out of turn?

BRINDSLEY: Not at all. I've told Carol all *about* Clea.

[*He bangs* CLEA *again, a little harder – who correspondingly bumps against* HAROLD.]

Though I must say, Harold, I'm surprised you call three months 'a long time'.

[CLEA *shoots him a look of total outrage at this lie.* HAROLD *is also astonished.*]

CAROL: What was she like?

BRINDSLEY [*meaningfully, into* CLEA's *ear*]: I suppose you can hardly remember her, Harold.

HAROLD [*speaking across her*]: Why on earth shouldn't I?

BRINDSLEY: Well, since it was two years ago, you've probably forgotten.

HAROLD: Two years?!

BRINDSLEY: *Two years ago!*

[*He punches* CLEA *so hard that the rebound knocks* HAROLD *off the sofa, drink and all.*]

HAROLD [*picking himself up. Spitefully*]: Well, now since you mention it, I remember her perfectly. I mean, she's not one you can easily forget!

CAROL: Was she pretty?

HAROLD: No, not at all. In fact, I'd say the opposite. Actually she was rather plain.

BRINDSLEY: She wasn't!

HAROLD: I'm just giving my opinion.

BRINDSLEY: You've never given it before.

HAROLD [*leaning over* CLEA]: I was never *asked*! But since it's come up, I always thought she was ugly. For one thing, she had teeth like a picket fence – yellow and spiky. And for another, she had bad skin.

BRINDSLEY: She had nothing of the kind!

HAROLD: She did. I remember it perfectly. It was like a new pink wallpaper, with an old grey crumbly paper underneath.

MISS FURNIVAL: Quite right, Mr Gorringe. I hardly ever saw her, but I do recall her skin. It was a strange colour, as you say – and very coarse . . . Not soft, as the skins of young ladies should be, if they *are* young ladies.

[CLEA *rises in outrage.*]

HAROLD: Aye, that's right. Coarse.

MISS FURNIVAL: And rather lumpy.

HAROLD: Very lumpy.

BRINDSLEY: This is disgraceful.

HAROLD: You knew I never liked her, Brindsley. She was too clever by half.

MISS FURNIVAL: And so tiresomely Bohemian.

CAROL: You mean she was as pretentious as her name?

[CLEA, *who has been reacting to this last exchange of comments about her like a spectator at a tennis match, now reacts to* CAROL *open-mouthed.*]

I bet she was. That photograph I found showed her in a dirndl and a sort of sultry peasant blouse. She looked like 'The Bartered Bride' done by Lloyds Bank.

[*They laugh,* BRINDSLEY *hardest of all. Guided by the noise,* CLEA *aims her hand and slaps his face.*]

BRINDSLEY: Ahh!

CAROL: What's wrong?

MISS FURNIVAL: What is it, Mr Miller?

BRINDSLEY [*furious*]: That's not very funny, Harold. What the hell's the matter with you?

[CLEA *makes her escape.*]

HAROLD [*indignant*]: With *me*?

BRINDSLEY: Well, I'm sure it wasn't the Colonel.

COLONEL: What wasn't, sir?

[BRINDSLEY, *groping about, catches* CLEA *by the bottom, and instantly recognizes it.*]

BRINDSLEY: Clea! . . . [*In horror*] Clea!!

[CLEA *breaks loose and moves away from him. During the following he tries to find her in the dark, and she narrowly avoids him.*]

COLONEL: What?

BRINDSLEY: I was just remembering her, sir. You're all talking the most awful nonsense. She was beautiful . . . And anyway, Harold, you just said I was famous for my taste in women.

HAROLD: Aye, but it had its lapses.

BRINDSLEY [*frantically moving about*]: Rubbish! She was beautiful and tender and considerate and kind and loyal and witty and adorable in every way!

CAROL: You told me she was as cosy as a steel razor-blade.

BRINDSLEY: Did I? Surely not! No. What I said was . . . something quite different . . . Utterly different . . . entirely different . . . As different as chalk from cheese. Although when you come to think of it, cheese isn't all that different from chalk! [*He gives his braying laugh.*]

COLONEL: Are you sure you know what you're talking about?

[*During this* CLEA *has reached the table, picked up a bottle of Scotch, and rejected it in favour of vodka, which she takes with her.*]

CAROL: You said to me in this room when I asked you what she was like, 'She was a painter. Very honest. Very clever, and just about as cosy –'

BRINDSLEY [*stopping, exasperated*]: As a steel razor-blade! Well then, I said it! So bloody what? . . .

CAROL: So nothing!

[*He throws out his hands in a gesture of desperate exhaustion and bumps straight into CLEA. They instantly embrace, CLEA twining herself around him, her vodka bottle held aloft. A tiny pause.*]

COLONEL: If that boy isn't touched, I don't know the meaning of the word!

CAROL: What's all this talk about her being kind and tender, all of a sudden?

BRINDSLEY [*tenderly, holding CLEA*]: She could be. On occasion. Very.

CAROL: Very rare occasions, I imagine.

BRINDSLEY: Not so rare. [*He kisses CLEA again.*] Not so rare at all.
[*He leads her softly past the irritated CAROL, towards the stairs.*]

CAROL: Meaning what, exactly? . . . [*Shouting*] Brindsley, I'm talking to you!

BRINDSLEY [*sotto voce, into CLEA's ear as they stand just behind HAROLD*]: I can explain. Go up to the bedroom. Wait for me there.

HAROLD [*in amazement: thinking he is being addressed*]: Now? . . . Do you think this is quite the moment?

BRINDSLEY: Oh God! . . . I wasn't talking to you!

CAROL: What did you say?

HAROLD [*to CAROL*]: I think he wants *you* upstairs. [*Slyly*] For what purpose, I can't begin to imagine.

COLONEL: They're going to do some more of that plotting, I dare say.

MISS FURNIVAL: Lover's talk, Colonel.

COLONEL: Very touching, I'm sure.

[BRINDSLEY *pushes* CLEA *ahead of him up the stairs.*]

MISS FURNIVAL: 'Journeys end in lovers meeting,' as my father always used to say.

COLONEL [*grimly*]: What a strikingly original father you seem to have had, madam!

[*CAROL joins the other two on the stairs. We see all three groping blindly up to the bedroom, BRINDSLEY's hands on CLEA's hips, CAROL's on BRINDSLEY's.*]

CAROL [*with a conspirator's stage whisper*]: What is it, darling? Has something gone wrong? What can't you move?

[*This next dialogue sotto voce.*]

BRINDSLEY: Nothing. It's all back – every bit of it – except the sofa, and I've covered that up.

CAROL: You mean, we can have lights?

BRINDSLEY: Yes... NO!!

CAROL: Why not?

BRINDSLEY: Never mind!

CAROL: Why do you want me in the bedroom?

BRINDSLEY: I don't! Go away!

CAROL: Charming!

BRINDSLEY: I didn't mean that.

COLONEL: There you are. They *are* plotting again. What the hell is going on up there?

BRINDSLEY: Nothing, Colonel. I've just remembered – there may be a torch under my bed. I keep it to blind the burglars with. Have another drink, Colonel!

[*He pushes CLEA into the bedroom and shuts the door.*]

COLONEL: What d'you mean another? I haven't had *one* yet.

MISS FURNIVAL: Oh! Poor Colonel! Let me get you one.

COLONEL [*rising*]: I can get one for myself, thank you. Let me get you another lemonade.

MISS FURNIVAL [*rising*]: No thank you, Colonel, I'll manage myself. It's good practice!

[*They grope towards the drinks table. Above, CLEA and BRINDSLEY sit on the bed.*]

CLEA: So this is what they mean by a blind date! What the hell is going on?

BRINDSLEY [*sarcastic*]: Nothing! Georg Bamberger is only coming to see my work tonight, and we've got a main fuse.

CLEA: Is that the reason for all this furtive clutching?

BRINDSLEY: Look, I can't explain things at the moment.

CLEA: Who's that – [*debutante accent*] 'frightful gel'?

BRINDSLEY: Just a friend.

CLEA: She sounded more than that.

BRINDSLEY: Well, if you must know, it's Carol. I've told you about her.

CLEA: The Idiot Deb?

BRINDSLEY: She's a very sweet girl. As a matter of fact we've become very good friends in the last six weeks.

CLEA: How good?

BRINDSLEY: Just good.

CLEA: And have you become friends with her father too?

BRINDSLEY: If it's any of your business, they just dropped in to meet Mr Bamberger.

CLEA: What was it you wanted to tell me on the phone tonight?

BRINDSLEY: Nothing.

CLEA: You're lying!

BRINDSLEY: Ah, here comes the inquisition! Look, Clea, if you ever loved me, just slip away quietly with no more questions, and I'll come round later and explain everything, I promise.

CLEA: I don't believe you.

BRINDSLEY: Please darling ... Please ... Please ... Please!!

[*They kiss, passionately, stretched out on the bed.*]

COLONEL [*pouring*]: At last ... a decent glass of Scotch. Are you getting your lemonade?

MISS FURNIVAL [*cheerfully pouring herself an enormous gin*]: Oh yes, thank you, Colonel!

COLONEL: I'm just wonderin' if this Bamberger fellow is goin' to show up at all. He's half an hour late already.

HAROLD: Oh! That's nothing, Colonel. Millionaires are always late. It's their thing.

MISS FURNIVAL: I'm sure you're right, Mr Gorringe, That's how *I* imagine them. Hands like silk, and always two hours late.

CAROL: Brin's been up there a long time. What can he be doing?

HAROLD: Maybe he's got that Clea hidden away in his bedroom, and they're having a tête-à-tête!!

CAROL: What a flagrant suggestion, Mr Gorringe.

BRINDSLEY [*disengaging himself*]: No one in the world kisses like you.

CLEA: I missed you so badly, Brin. I had to see you. I've thought about nothing else these past six weeks. Brin, I made the most awful mistake walking out.

BRINDSLEY: Clea – *please!*

CLEA: I mean we've known each other for four years. We can't just throw each other away like old newspapers.

BRINDSLEY: I don't see why not. You know my politics, you've heard my gossip, and you've certainly been through all my entertainment section.

CLEA: Well, how about a second edition?

BRINDSLEY: Darling, we simply can't talk about this now. Can't you trust me just for an hour?

CLEA: Of course I can, darling. You don't want me down there?

BRINDSLEY: No.

CLEA: Then I'll get undressed and go quietly to bed. When you've got rid of them all, I'll be waiting.

BRINDSLEY: That's a terrible idea!

CLEA [*reaching for him*]: I think it's lovely. A little happy relaxation for us both.

BRINDSLEY [*falling off the bed*]: I'm perfectly relaxed!

CAROL: Brindsley!

CLEA: 'Too solemn for day, too sweet for night. Come not in darkness, come not in light.' That's me, isn't it?

BRINDSLEY: Of course not. I just can't explain now, that's all.

CLEA: Oh, very well, you can explain later . . . in bed!

BRINDSLEY: Not tonight, Clea.

CLEA: Either that or I come down and discover your sordid secret.

BRINDSLEY: There *is* no sordid secret!

CLEA: Then you won't mind my coming down!

CAROL, COLONEL [*roaring together*]: BRINDSLEY!!!

BRINDSLEY: Oh God!! ... All right, stay. Only keep quiet ... Blackmailing bitch! [*He emerges at the top of the stairs.*] Yes, my sweet?

CAROL: What are you doing up there? You've been an eternity!

BRINDSLEY: I ... I ... I'm just looking in the bathroom, my darling. You never know what you might find in that clever little cabinet!

COLONEL [*moving to the stairs*]: Are you trying to madden me, sir? Are you trying to put me in a fury?

BRINDSLEY: Certainly not, sir!!

COLONEL: I warn you, Miller, it's not difficult! In the old days in the regiment I was known for my furies! I was famous for my furies! ... Do you hear?

CLEA: I may sing! [*She goes off into the bathroom.*]

BRINDSLEY: I may knock your teeth in!

COLONEL: What did you say?

CAROL: Brin! How dare you talk to Daddy like that!

BRINDSLEY: Oh!! I ... I ... I wasn't talking to Daddy like that ...

CAROL: Then who *were* you talking to?

BRINDSLEY: I was talking to no one! Myself I was talking to! I was saying ... 'If I keep groping about up here like this, I might knock my teeth in!'

COLONEL: Mad! ... Mad! ... Mad as the south wind! It's the only explanation – you've got yourself engaged to a lunatic.

CAROL: There's something going on up there, and I'm coming up to find out what it is. Do you hear me, Brin?

BRINDSLEY: Carol – no!

CAROL [*climbing the stairs*]: I'm not such a fool as you take me for. I know when you're hiding something. Your voice goes all deceitful – very, very foxipegs!

BRINDSLEY: Darling please. That's not very ladylike ... I'm sure the Colonel won't approve of you entering a man's bedroom in the dark!

[*Enter* SCHUPPANZIGH. *He wears the overcoat and peaked cap of the London Electricity Board and carries a large tool-bag, similarly labelled.*]

CAROL: I'm comin' up, Brindsley, I'm comin' up!!!

BRINDSLEY [*scrambling down*]: I'm coming down ... We'll all have a nice cosy drink ...

SCHUPPANZIGH [*German accent*]: 'Allo please? Mr Miller? Mr Miller? I've come as was arranged.

BRINDSLEY: My God ... it's Bamberger!

CAROL: Bamberger?

BRINDSLEY: Yes, Bamberger. [BRINDSLEY *rushes down the remaining stairs, pulling* CAROL *with him.*]

SCHUPPANZIGH: You must have thought I was never coming! [*He takes off his overcoat and cap.*]

BRINDSLEY: Not at all. I'm delighted you could spare the time. I know how busy you are. I'm afraid we've had the most idiotic disaster. We've had a fuse.

HAROLD: You'll have to speak up, dear, He's stone deaf!

BRINDSLEY [*yelling*]: We've had a fuse – not the best conditions for seeing sculpture.

SCHUPPANZIGH: Please not to worry. Here!

[*He produces a torch from his pocket and 'lights' it. The light on stage dims a little, as usual, to indicate this. All relax with audible sighs of pleasure.* SCHUPPANZIGH *at once places his tool-bag on the Regency chair, and puts his coat and cap on top of it, concealing the fact that it is one of* HAROLD'*s chairs.*]

CAROL: Oh, what a relief!

BRINDSLEY [*hastily dragging the sheet over the rest of the sofa*]: Do you always travel with a torch?

SCHUPPANZIGH: Mostly, yes. It helps to see details. [*Seeing the others*] You are holding a private view?.

MISS FURNIVAL: Oh no! I was just going, I'd hate to distract you.

SCHUPPANZIGH: Please not on my account, dear lady, I am not so easily distracted.

MISS FURNIVAL [*charmed*]: Oh! ...

184

BRINDSLEY [*yelling in his ear*]: May I present Colonel Melkett?

COLONEL [*yelling in his other ear*]: A great honour, sir!

SCHUPPANZIGH [*banging his ear, to clear it*]: No, no, mine – mine!

BRINDSLEY: Miss Carol Melkett!

CAROL [*screeching in his ear*]: I say: hello. So glad you got here! It's terribly kind of you to take such an interest!

SCHUPPANZIGH: Not at all. *Vous êtes très gentil.*

CAROL [*yelling*]: What would you like to drink?

SCUPPANZIGH [*bewildered*]: A little vodka, would be beautiful!

CAROL: Of course!

BRINDSLEY: Harold Gorringe – a neighbour of mine!

HAROLD [*shouting*]: How do? Very honoured, I'm sure.

SCHUPPANZIGH: Enchanted.

HAROLD: I must say it's a real thrill, meeting you!

BRINDSLEY: And another neighbour, Miss Furnival!

SCHUPPANZIGH: Enchanted.

MISS FURNIVAL [*hooting in his ear*]: I'm afraid we've all been taking refuge from the *storm*, as it were. [*Exclaiming as she holds* SCHUPPANZIGH's *hand.*] Oh! It *is* true! They *are* softer! Much, much softer!

SCHUPPANZIGH [*utterly confused as she strokes his hand*]: Softer? Please?

[BRINDSLEY *and* HAROLD *pull her away, and she subsides onto the sofa.*]

BRINDSLEY: Miss Furnival, please!

CAROL [*at the drinks table*]: Darling, where's the vodka?

BRINDSLEY: It's on the table.

CAROL: No, it isn't.

BRINDSLEY: It must be!

[*Above,* CLEA *re-enters wearing the top half of* BRINDSLEY's *pajamas and nothing else. She gets into bed, still clutching the vodka bottle and carrying a plastic toothmug.*]

CAROL: Well, see for yourself. There's Winnie and Ginette, and Vera has quite vanished, the naughty girl!

BRINDSLEY: She can't have done.

SCHUPPANZIGH: Please don't concern yourselves. I am pressed for time. If I might just be shown where to go.

BRINDSLEY: Of course. It's through the studio there. Darling, if you would just show our guest into the studio – *with his torch.*

CAROL: What??...

BRINDSLEY [*sotto voce*]: *The sofa!* ... Get him out of here!

CAROL: Oh yes!!...

SCHUPPANZIGH [*sighting the sculpture*]: Oh! Good gracious! What an extraordinary object!

BRINDSLEY: Oh, that's just a spare piece of my work I keep in here!

SCHUPPANZIGH: Spare, maybe, but fascinating!

BRINDSLEY: You really think so?

SCHUPPANZIGH [*approaching it*]: I do! Ja!

BRINDSLEY: Well, in that case you should see my main collection. It's next door. My fianceé will show you!

[MISS FURNIVAL *sits on the sofa. She is now quite drunk.*]

SCHUPPANZIGH: One amazement at a time, if you please! In this gluttonous age it is easy to get visual indigestion – hard to find visual Alka Seltzer ... Permit me to digest this first!

BRINDSLEY: Oh, by all means ... Good, yes ... There's no hurry – no hurry at all ... Only ... [*Inspired*] Why don't you digest it *in the dark?*

SCHUPPANZIGH: I beg your pardon?

BRINDSLEY: You'll never believe it, sir, but I actually made that piece to be appreciated in the dark. I was working on a very interesting theory. You know how the Victorians said, 'Children should be seen and not heard'? Well, I say, 'Art should be felt and not seen.'

SCHUPPANZIGH: Amazing.

BRINDSLEY: Yes, isn't it. I call it my theory of Factual Tactility. If it doesn't stab you to the quick – it's not art. Look! Why don't you give me that torch, and try for yourself?

SCHUPPANZIGH: Very well, I will!! [*He hands* BRINDSLEY *the torch.*]

BRINDSLEY: Thank you!

[*He turns off the torch and hands it to* CAROL. *At the same moment* MISS FURNIVAL *quietly lies down, her full length on the sofa.*]

Now just stretch out your arms and feel it all over, sir. [*He steals towards the studio.*] Have a good long feel!

[SCHUPPANZIGH *embraces the metal sculpture with a fervent clash. He pulls at the two metal prongs.*]

Do you see what I mean? [*Silently he opens the curtains.*]

SCHUPPANZIGH: Amazing! . . . Absolutely incredible! . . . It's quite true . . . Like this, the piece becomes a masterpiece at once.

BRINDSLEY [*astonished*]: It does??

SCHUPPANZIGH: But of course! I feel it here – and here – the two needles of man's unrest! . . . Self-love and self-hate, leading to the same point! That's the meaning of the work, isn't it?

BRINDSLEY: Of course. You've got it in one! You're obviously a great expert, sir!

[*Quietly he pulls the sofa into the studio, bearing on it the supine* MISS FURNIVAL, *who waves good-bye as she disappears.*]

SCHUPPANZIGH: Not at all. *Vous êtes très gentil* – but it is evident! . . . Standing here in the dark, one can feel the vital thrust of the argument! The essential anguish! The stress and the torment of our times! It is simple but not simple-minded! Ingenious, but not ingenuous! Above all, it has real moral force! Of how many modern works can one say that, good people?

CAROL: Oh, none, none at all really!

SCHUPPANZIGH: I hope I do not lecture. It can be a fault with me.

CAROL: Not at all! I could listen all night, it's so profound.

HAROLD: Me too. Really deep!

COLONEL: I don't know anything about this myself, sir, but it's an honour to listen to you.

[*He starts off upstage in search of the sofa, seating himself tentatively in the air, then moving himself along in a sitting position, trying to find it with his rear end. At the same moment* BRINDSLEY *emerges from the studio, closes the curtains behind him, and gropes his way to the upstage corner where there stands a small packing case. This he carried forward, hopefully to do duty for the missing sofa. Just as he places it on the ground the travelling* COLONEL *sits on it, trapping* BRINDSLEY'*s hand beneath his weight. During the following,* BRINDSLEY *tries frantically to free himself.*]

SCHUPPANZIGH: *Vous êtes très gentil!*

HAROLD: You mean to say you see all that in a bit of metal?

SCHUPPANZIGH: A *tiny* bit of metal, that's the point. A miracle of compression! You want my opinion, this boy is a genius. A master of the miniature. In the space of a matchbox he can realize anything he wants – the black virginity of Chartres! The white chorale of the Acropolis! *Wunderbar!*

CAROL: Oh how super!

SCHUPPANZIGH: You should charge immense sums for work like this, Mr Miller. They should be very very expensive! This one, for example, how much is this?

BRINDSLEY: Fifty –

CAROL: Five hundred guineas!

SCHUPPANZIGH: Ah so! Very cheap.

HAROLD: Cheap!

CAROL: I think so, Mr Gorringe. Well . . . so will you have it then?

SCHUPPANZIGH: Me?

BRINDSLEY: Darling . . . aren't you rushing things just a little? Perhaps you would like to see the rest of my work.

SCHUPPANZIGH: Alas, I have no more time. To linger would be pleasant, but alas, I must work . . . Also, as Moses discovered, it is sufficient to glimpse milk and honey. One does not have to wolf them down!

BRINDSLEY: Well.

COLONEL: Well . . .

HAROLD: Well . . . .

CAROL: Well . . . Would you like it then?

SCHUPPANZIGH: Very much.

COLONEL [*rising.* BRINDSLEY *is freed at last*]: For five hundred guineas?

SCHUPPANZIGH: Certainly – if I had it!

HAROLD: According to the Sunday paper, you must be worth at least seventeen million pounds.

SCHUPPANZIGH: The Sunday papers are notoriously ill-informed. According to my bank statement, I was worth one hundred pounds, eight shillings and fourpence.

HAROLD: You mean you've gone broke?

SCHUPPANZIGH: No. I mean I never had any more.

COLONEL: Now look, sir, I know millionaires are supposed to be eccentric, but this is gettin' tiresome.

CAROL: Daddy, ssh! –

SCHUPPANZIGH: Millionaires? Who do you think I am?

COLONEL: Dammit, man! – You must know who you are!

CAROL: Mr Bamberger, is this some kind of joke you like to play?

SCHUPPANZIGH: Excuse me. That is not my name.

BRINDSLEY: It isn't?

SCHUPPANZIGH: No. My name is Schuppanzigh. Franz Schuppanzigh. Born in Weimar 1905. Student of philosophy at Heidelberg, 1934. Refugee to this country, 1938. Regular employment ever since with the London Electricity Board!

[*All rise.*]

CAROL: Electricity?

MISS FURNIVAL: Electricity!

BRINDSLEY: You mean you're not? –

HAROLD: Of course he's not!

SCHUPPANZIGH: But who did you imagine I was?

HAROLD [*furious*]: How dare you? [*He snatches the electrician's torch.*]

SCHUPPANZIGH [*retreating before him*]: Please? –

HAROLD: Of all the nerve, coming in here, giving us a lecture about needles and virgins, and all the time you're simply here to mend the fuses!

COLONEL: I agree with you, sir. It's monstrous!

SCHUPPANZIGH [*bewildered*]: It is?

[*The* COLONEL *takes the torch and shines it pitilessly in the man's face.*]

COLONEL: You come in here, a public servant, and proceed to harangue your employers, unasked and uninvited.

SCHUPPANZIGH [*bewildered*]: Excuse me. But I *was* invited.

COLONEL: Don't answer back. In my day you would have been fired on the spot for impertinence.

CAROL: Daddy's absolutely right! Ever since the Beatles, the lower classes think they can behave exactly as they want.

COLONEL [*handing the torch to* BRINDSLEY]: Miller, will you kindly show this feller his work?

BRINDSLEY: The mains are in the cellar. There's a trap-door. [*Indicating*] Do you mind?

SCHUPPANZIGH [*snatching the torch furiously*]: Why should I mind? It's why I came, after all! [*He takes his coat, cap and bag off* HAROLD's *Regency chair . . . Seeing it*] Now there is a really beautiful chair!

  [BRINDSLEY *stares at the chair aghast – and in a twinkling seats himself in it to conceal it.*]

BRINDSLEY [*exasperated*]: Why don't you just go into the cellar?

SCHUPPANZIGH: *How?* Where is it?

BRINDSLEY [*to* CAROL]: Darling, will you open the trap, please.

CAROL: Me? [*Understanding – as he indicates the chair*] Oh – yes! [*She kneels and struggles to open the trap.*]

COLONEL [*to* BRINDSLEY]: Well, I must say, that's very gallant of you, Miller.

BRINDSLEY: I've got a sudden touch of lumbago, sir. It often afflicts me after long spells in the dark.

CAROL [*very sympathetic*]: Oh, darling! Has it come back?

BRINDSLEY: I'm afraid it has, my sweet.

HAROLD [*opening the trap*]: Here, let me. I'm not as frail as our wilting friend. [*To* SCHUPPANZIGH] Well, down you go, you!

SCHUPPANZIGH [*shrugging*]: So. Farewell. I leave the light of Art for the dark of Science.

HAROLD: Let's have a little less of your lip, shall we?

SCHUPPANZIGH: Excuse me.

  [SCHUPPANZIGH *descends through the trap, taking the torch with him.* HAROLD *slams the trap-door down irritably after him, and of course the lights immediately come up full. There is a long pause. All stand about embarrassed. Suddenly they hear the noise of* MISS FURNIVAL *singing 'Rock of Ages' in a high drunken voice from behind the curtain. Above, attracted by the noise of the slam,* CLEA *gets out of bed, still clutching the vodka and toothmug. opens the door, and stands at the top of the stairs listening.*]

BRINDSLEY: None of this evening is happening.

CAROL: Cheer up, darling. In a few minutes everything will be all right. Mr Bamberger will arrive in the light – he'll adore your work and give you twenty thousand pounds for your whole collection.

BRINDSLEY [*sarcastic*]: Oh, yes!

CAROL: Then we can buy a super Georgian house and live what's laughingly known as happily ever after. I want to leave this place just as soon as we're married.

[CLEA *hears this. Her mouth opens wide.*]

BRINDSLEY [*nervously*]: Sssh!

CAROL: Why? I don't want to live in a slum for our first couple of years – like other newlyweds.

BRINDSLEY: Sssh! Ssssh!...

CAROL: What's the matter with you?

BRINDSLEY: The gods listen, darling. They're given me a terrible night so far. They may do worse.

CAROL [*cooing*]: I know, darling. You've had a filthy evening. Poor babykins. But I'll fight them with you. I don't care a fig for those naughty old Goddipegs! [*Looking up*] Do you hear? Not a single little fig!

[CLEA *aims at the voice and sends a jet of vodka splashing down over* CAROL.]

Ahh!!!

BRINDSLEY: What is it?

CAROL: It's raining!

BRINDSLEY: Don't be ridiculous.

CAROL: I'm all wet!

BRINDSLEY: How can you be?

[CLEA *throws vodka over a wider area.* HAROLD *gets it.*]

HAROLD: Hey, what's going on?

BRINDSLEY: What?

COLONEL: What the devil's the matter with you all? What are you hollerin' for? [*He gets a slug of vodka in the face.*] Ahh!!

BRINDSLEY [*inspired*]: It's a leak – the water mains must have gone now.

HAROLD: Oh good God!

BRINDSLEY: It must be!

[*Mischievously,* CLEA *raps her bottle loudly on the top stair. There is a terrified silence. All look up.*]

HAROLD: Don't say there's someone else here.

BRINDSLEY: Good Lord!

COLONEL: Who's there?

[*Silence from above.*]

Come on! I know you're there!

BRINDSLEY [*improvising wildly*]: I – I bet you it's Mrs Punnet.

[CLEA *looks astonished.*]

COLONEL: Who?

BRINDSLEY [*for* CLEA's *benefit*]: Mrs Punnet. My cleaning woman.

HAROLD: Cleaning woman?

BRINDSLEY: She does for me on Mondays, Wednesdays and Fridays.

CAROL: Well, what would she be doing here now?

BRINDSLEY: I've just remembered – she rang up and said she'd look in about six to tidy up the place.

COLONEL: Dammit, man, it's almost eleven.

HAROLD: She's not that conscientious. She couldn't be!

CAROL: Not these days!

COLONEL: Well, we'll soon see. [*Calling up*] Mrs Punnet?

BRINDSLEY [*desperately*]: Don't interrupt her, sir. She doesn't like to be disturbed when she's working. Why don't we just leave her to potter around upstairs with her duster?

COLONEL: Let us first just see if it's her. Is that you, Mrs Punnet? ...
  [CLEA *keeps still*.]

COLONEL [*roaring*]: MRS PUNNET!

CLEA [*deciding on a cockney voice of great antiquity*]: 'Allo! Yes?

BRINDSLEY [*weakly*]: It is. Good heavens, Mrs Punnet, what on earth are you doing up there?

CLEA: I'm just giving your bedroom a bit of a tidy, sir.

BRINDSLEY: At this time of night?

  [*The mischief in* CLEA *begins to take over.*]

CLEA: Better late than never, sir, as they say. I know how you like your bedroom to be nice and inviting when you're giving one of your parties.

BRINDSLEY: Yes, yes, yes, of course ...

COLONEL: When did you come, madam?

CLEA: Just a few minutes ago, sir. I didn't like to disturb you, so I come on up 'ere.

HAROLD: Was it you pouring all that water on us, then?

CLEA: Water? Good 'eavens, I must have upset something. It's as black as Newgate's Knocker up 'ere. Are you playing one of your saucy games, Mr Miller?

BRINDSLEY: No, Mrs Punnet. We've had a fuse. It's all over the house.

CLEA: Oh! A *fuse!* I thought it might be one of them saucy games in the dark, sir: Sardines or Piccadilly. The kind that end in a general squeeze-up. I know you're rather partial to kinky games, Mr Miller, so I just wondered. [*She starts to come down the stairs.*]

BRINDSLEY [*distinctly*]: It is a fuse, Mrs Punnet. The man's mending it now. The lights will be on *any minute!*

CLEA: Well, that'll be a relief for you, won't it? [*She dashes the vodka accurately in his face, passes him by and comes into the room.*]

BRINDSLEY: Yes, of course. Now why don't you just go on home?

CLEA: I'm sorry I couldn't come before, sir. I was delayed, you see. My Rosie's been taken queer again.

BRINDSLEY: I quite understand! [*He gropes around trying to hide her, but she continuously evades him.*]

CLEA [*relentlessly*]: It's her tummy. There's a lump under her belly button the size of a grapefruit.

HAROLD: Oh, how nasty!

CLEA: Horrid. Poor little Rosie. I said to her this evening, I said, 'There's no good your being mulish, my girl. You're going to the hospital first thing tomorrow morning and getting yourself ultra-violated!'

BRINDSLEY: Well, hadn't you better be getting back to poor little Rosie! She must need you, surely? – And there's really nothing you can do here tonight.

CLEA [*meaningfully*]: Are you sure of that, sir?

BRINDSLEY: Positive, thank you.

[*They are close now.*]

CLEA: I mean, I know what this place can be like after one of your evenings. A gypsy caravan isn't in it. Gin bottles all over the floor! Bras and panties in the sink! And God knows what in the –

[BRINDSLEY *muzzles her with his hand. She bites it hard, and he drops to his knees in silent agony.*]

COLONEL: Please watch what you say, madam. You don't know it, but you're in the presence of Mr Miller's fiancée.

CLEA: Fiancée?

COLONEL: Yes, and I am her father.

CLEA: Well, I never ... Oh, Mr Miller! I'm so 'appy for you! ... Fiancée! Oh sir!, And you never *told* me!

BRINDSLEY: I was keeping it a surprise.

CLEA: Well, I never! Oh, how lovely! ... May I kiss you sir, please?

BRINDSLEY [*on his knees*]: Well, yes, yes, of course ...

[CLEA *gropes for his ear, finds it and twists it.*]

CLEA: Oh sir, I'm so pleased for you! And for *you*, Miss, too!

CAROL: Thank you.

CLEA [*to* COLONEL MELKETT]: And for *you*, sir.

COLONEL: Thank you.

CLEA: You must be Miss Clea's father.

COLONEL: Miss Clea? I don't understand.

[*Triumphantly she sticks out her tongue at* BRINDSLEY, *who collapses his length on the floor, face down, in a gesture of total surrender. For him it is the end. The evening can hold no further disasters for him.*]

CLEA [*to* CAROL]: Well, I never! So you've got him at last! Well done, Miss Clea! I never thought you would – not after four years . . .

BRINDSLEY: No – no – no – no . . .

CLEA: Forgive me, sir, if I'm speaking out of turn, but you must admit four years is a long time to be courting one woman. Four days is stretching it a bit nowadays!

BRINDSLEY [*weakly*]: Mrs Punnet, *please!*

CAROL: Four years!

CLEA: Well, yes, dear. It's been all of that and a bit more really, hasn't it? [*In a stage whisper*] And of course it's just in time. It was getting a bit prominent, your little bun in the oven.

[CAROL *screeches with disgust.* BRINDSLEY *covers his ears.*]

Oh, Miss, I don't mean that's why he popped the question. Of course it's not. He's always been stuck on you. He told me so, not one week ago, in this room. [*Sentimentally*] 'Mrs Punnet,' he says, 'Mrs Punnet, as far as I'm concerned you can keep the rest of them – Miss Clea will always be on top of the heap for me.' 'Oh,' I says,' then what about that debutante bit, Carol, the one's you're always telling me about?' 'Oh, 'er,' he says, 'she's just a bit of Knightsbridge candyfloss. A couple of licks and you've 'ad 'er.'

[*There is a long pause.* CLEA *is now sitting on the table, swinging her vodka bottle in absolute command of the situation.*]

COLONEL [*faintly; at last grappling with the situation*]: Did you say four years, madam?

CLEA [*in her own voice, quiet*]: Yes, Colonel. Four years, in this room.

HAROLD: I know that voice. It's Clea!

MISS FURNIVAL [*surprised*]: Clea!

CAROL [*horrified*]: Clea!

BRINDSLEY [*unconvincingly*]: Clea!

CLEA: Surprised, Brin?

CAROL [*understanding*]: Clea! . . .

COLONEL: I don't understand anything that's going on in this room!

CLEA: I know. It is a very odd room, isn't it? It's like a magic dark room, where everything happens the wrong way round. Rain falls indoors, the Daily comes at night, and turns in a second from a nice maid into nasty mistress.

BRINDSLEY: Be quiet, Clea!

CLEA: At last! One real word of protest! Having you finished lying, then? Have you eaten the last crumb of humble pie? Oh you coward, you bloody coward! Just because you didn't want to marry me, did you have to settle for this lot?

CAROL: Marry!

COLONEL: Marry?

CLEA: Four years of meaning to end in this triviality! Miss Laughingly-Known-As and her Daddipegs!

CAROL: Stop her! She's disgusting!

COLONEL: How can I, for God's sake?

CAROL: Well, where's all that bloody resource you keep talking about?

[*The* COLONEL *goes to her but takes* CLEA's *hand by mistake.*]

COLONEL: Now calm down, Dumpling. Keep your head . . . There – hold my hand, that's it, now Daddy's here. Everything is under control. All right?

CLEA: Are you sure that is your daughter's hand you're holding, Colonel?

COLONEL: What? Carol, isn't this your hand?

CAROL: No.

CLEA: You must have lived with your daughter for well over twenty years, Colonel. What remarkable use you've made of your eyes.

[*There is another pause. The* COLONEL *moves away in embarrassment.*]

CLEA [*wickedly*]: All right! Kinky game time! . . . Let's all play Guess the Hand.

HAROLD: Oh good God!

CLEA: Or would you rather Guess the Lips, Harold?

CAROL: How disgusting!

CLEA: Well, that's me, dear. [CAROL's *accent*] I'm Queen Disgusti-pegs! [*She seizes* CAROL's *hand and puts it into* HAROLD's.] Who's that?

CAROL: I don't know.

CLEA: Guess.

CAROL: I don't know, and I don't care.

CLEA: Oh go on. Have a go!

CAROL: It's Brin, of course: You can't trick me like that! It's Brind-sley's stupid hand.

HAROLD: I'm afraid you're wrong. It's me.

CAROL [*struggling*]: It's not. You're lying.

HAROLD [*holding on*]: I'm not. I don't lie.

CAROL: You're lying! . . . You're lying!

HAROLD: I'm not.

[CAROL *breaks away and blunders upstage. She is becoming hysterical.*]

CLEA: You try it, Harold. Take the hand on your right.

HAROLD: I'm not playing. It's a bloody silly game.

CLEA: Go on . . . [*She seizes his hand and puts it into* BRINDSLEY's.] Well?

HAROLD: It's Brin.

BRINDSLEY: Yes.

CLEA: Well done! [*She sits on the low stool.*]

CAROL [*outraged*]: How does he know that? How does *he* know your hand and I don't?

BRINDSLEY: Calm down, Carol.

CAROL: Answer me! I want to know!

BRINDSLEY: Stop it!

CAROL: I won't!

BRINDSLEY: You're getting hysterical!

CAROL: Leave me alone! I want to go home.

[*And suddenly* MISS FURNIVAL *gives a sharp short scream and blunders out through the curtains.*]

197

MISS FURNIVAL: Prams! Prams! Prams – in the supermarket! . . .

[*They all freeze. She is evidently out of control in a world of her own fears. She speaks quickly and strangely.*]

All those hideous wire prams full of babies and bottles – 'Cornflakes over there' is all they say – and then they leave you to yourself. Biscuits over there – cat food over there – fish cakes over there – Airwick over there! Pink stamps, green stamps, free balloons – television dinners – pay as you go out – oh, Daddy, it's *awful*! . . . And then the Godless ones, the heathens in their leather jackets – laughing me to scorn! But not for long. Oh, no! Who shall stand when He appeareth? He'll strike them from their motor-cycles! He'll dash their helmets to the ground! Yes, verily, I say unto thee – there shall be an end of gasoline! An end to cigarette puffing and jostling with hips . . . Keep off . . . Keep off! Keep off! . . .

[*She runs drunkenly across the room and collides with* HAROLD.]

HAROLD: Come on, Ferny, I think it's time we went home.

MISS FURNIVAL [*pulling herself together*]: Yes. You're quite right . . .

[*With an attempt at grandeur*] I'm sorry I can't stay any longer, Mr Miller; but your millionaire is unpardonably late. So typical of modern manners . . . Express my regrets, if you please.

BRINDSLEY: Certainly.

[*Leaning heavily on* HAROLD's *arm she leaves the room. He shuts the door after them.*]

Thank you, Clea. Thank you very much.

CLEA: Any time.

BRINDSLEY: You had no right.

CLEA: No?

BRINDSLEY: *You* walked out on *me*. [*He joins her on the low stool.*]

CLEA: Is that what I did?

BRINDSLEY: You said you never wanted to see me again.

CLEA: I never saw you at all – how could you be walked out on? You should *live* in the dark, Brindsley. It's your natural element.

BRINDSLEY: Whatever that means.

CLEA: It means you don't really want to be seen. Why is that,

Brindsley? Do you think if someone really saw you, they would never love you?

BRINDSLEY: Oh, go away.

CLEA: I want to know.

BRINDSLEY: Yes, you always want to know. Pick–pick–pick away! Why is *that*, Clea? Have you ever thought why you need to do it? Well?

CLEA: Perhaps because I care about you.

BRINDSLEY: Perhaps there's nothing to care about. Just a fake artist.

CLEA: Stop pitying yourself. It's always your vice. I told you when I met you: you could either be a good artist, or a chic fake. You didn't like it, because I refused just to give you applause.

BRINDSLEY: God knows, you certainly did that!

CLEA: Is that what *she* gives you? Twenty hours of ego-massage every day?

BRINDSLEY: At least our life together isn't the replica of the Holy Inquisition you made of ours. I didn't have an affair with you: it was just four years of nooky with Torquemada!

CLEA: And don't say you didn't enjoy it!

BRINDSLEY: Enjoy it? I hated every second of it.

CLEA: Yes, I remember.

BRINDSLEY: Every second!

CLEA: I recall.

BRINDSLEY: When you left for Finland, it was the happiest day of my life.

CLEA: Mine, too!

BRINDSLEY: I sighed with relief.

CLEA: So did I.

BRINDSLEY: I went out dancing that very night.

CLEA: So did I. It was out with the lyre and the timbrel.

BRINDSLEY: Good. Then that's all right.

CLEA: Fine.

BRINDSLEY: Super!

CLEA: Duper!

BRINDSLEY: It's lovely to see you looking so happy.

CLEA: You too. Radiant with self-fulfilment.

[*A pause.*]

BRINDSLEY: If you felt like this, why did you come back?

CLEA: If *you* felt like this, why did you tell Mrs Punnet I was still at the top of the heap?

BRINDSLEY: I never said that!

CLEA: You did.

BRINDSLEY: Never!

CLEA: You *did!*

BRINDSLEY: Of course I didn't. You invented that ten minutes ago, when you were *playing* Mrs Punnet.

CLEA: I – Oh! So I did! . . .

[*They both giggle. She falls happily against his shoulder.*]

BRINDSLEY: You know something – I'm not sure she's not right.

[*During this exchange the* COLONEL *and his* DAUGHTER *have been standing frozen with astonished anger. Now the outraged father takes over. He is very angry.*]

COLONEL: No doubt this is very funny to you two.

CLEA: It is, quite, actually.

COLONEL: I'm not so easily amused, however, madam.

BRINDSLEY: Now look, Colonel –

COLONEL: Hold your tongue, sir, I'm talking. Do you know what would have happened to a young man in my day who dared to treat a girl the way you have treated my Dumpling?

BRINDSLEY: Well, I assume, Colonel –

COLONEL: Hold your tongue, I'm talking!

CAROL: Oh, leave it, Daddy. Let's just go home.

COLONEL: In a moment, Dumpling. Kindly leave this to me.

BRINDSLEY: Look, Carol, I can explain –

CAROL: Explain what?

BRINDSLEY: It's impossible here.

COLONEL: You understate, sir.

BRINDSLEY: Carol, you don't understand.

CAROL: What the hell's there to understand? All the time you were going with me, she was in the background – that's all there is to it – What were you doing? Weighing us up? ... Here! [*She pulls off her engagement ring.*]

BRINDSLEY: What?

CAROL: Your ring. Take the bloody thing back!

[*She throws it. It hits the* COLONEL *in the eye.*]

COLONEL: My eye! My damned eye!

[CLEA *starts to laugh again.*]

[*In mounting fury, clutching his eye.*] Oh very droll, madam! Very droll indeed! Laugh your fill! Miller! I asked you a question. Do you know what would have happened to a young lout like you in my day?

BRINDSLEY: Happened, sir?

COLONEL [*quietly*]: You'd have been thrashed, sir.

BRINDSLEY [*nervous*]: Thrashed –

[*The man of war begins to go after him, feeling his way in the dark – like some furious robot.*]

COLONEL: You'd have felt the mark of a father's horsewhip across your seducer's shoulders. You'd have gone down on your cad's bended knees, and begged my daughter's pardon for the insults you've offered her tonight.

BRINDSLEY [*retreating before the* COLONEL'*s groping advance*]: Would I, sir?

COLONEL: You'd have raised your guttersnipe voice in a piteous scream for mercy and forgiveness!

[*A terrible scream is indeed heard from the hall. They freeze, listening as it comes nearer and nearer, then the door is flung open and* HAROLD *plunges into the room. He is wild-eyed with rage: a lit and bent taper shakes in his furious hand.*]

HAROLD: Ooooooh! You villain!

BRINDSLEY: Harold –

HAROLD: You skunky, conniving little villain!

BRINDSLEY: What's the matter?

HAROLD [*raging*]: Have you seen the state of my room? My room? My lovely room, the most elegant and cared for in this entire district? – one chair turned absolutely upside down, one chair on top of another like a Portobello junk-shop! And that's not all, is it Brindsley? Oh no, that's not the worst by a long chalk, is it Brindsley?

BRINDSLEY: Long chalk?

HAROLD: Don't play the innocent with me. I thought I had a friend living all these years. I didn't know I was living opposite a Light-fingered Lenny!

BRINDSLEY: Harold! –

HAROLD [*hysterical*]: This is my reward, isn't it? – After years of looking after you, sweeping and tidying up this place, because you're too much of a slut to do it for yourself – to have my best pieces stolen from me to impress your new girl friend and her daddy. Or did she help you?

BRINDSLEY: Harold, it was an emergency.

HAROLD: Don't talk to me: I don't want to know! I know what you think of me now . . . 'Don't tell Harold about the engagement. He's not to be trusted. He's not a friend. He's just someone to steal things from!'

BRINDSLEY: You know that's not true.

HAROLD [*shrieking – in one hysterical breath*]: I know I was the last one to know – that's what I know! I have to find it out in a room full of strangers. Me, who's listened to more of your miseries in the small hours of the morning than anyone else would put up with! All your boring talk about women, hour after hour, as if no one's got troubles but you! –

CLEA: She's getting hysterical, dear. Ignore her.

HAROLD: It's you who's going to be ignored, Clea. [*To* BRINDSLEY] As for you, all I can say about your engagement is this: you deserve each other, you and that little nit.

[CAROL *gives a shriek.*]

BRINDSLEY: Carol!

HAROLD: Oh, so you're there, are you? – Skulking in the shadows!

BRINDSLEY; Leave her alone!

HAROLD: I'm not going to touch her. I just want my things and I'll be off. Did you hear me, Brindsley? You give me my things now, or I'll call the police.

BRINDSLEY: Don't be ridiculous.

HAROLD [*grimly*]: Item: One lyre-back Regency chair, in lacquered mahogany with ormolu inlay and appliqué work on the cushions.

BRINDSLEY: In front of you.

[*Harold thrusts the taper at it to see it.*]

HAROLD: Ta. Item: One half-back sofa – likewise Regency – supported by claw legs and upholstered in a rich silk of bottle green to match the aforesaid chair.

BRINDSLEY: In the studio.

HAROLD: Unbelievable! Item: One Coalport vase, dated 1809, decorated on the rim with a pleasing design of daisies and peonies.

BRINDSLEY: On the floor.

HAROLD: Ta.

[BRINDSLEY *hands it to him.*]

Ooooh! You've even taken the flowers! I'll come back for the chair and sofa in a minute. [*Drawing himself up with all the offended dignity of which a* HAROLD GORRINGE *is capable.*] This is the end of our relationship, Brindsley. We won't be speaking again, I don't think.

[*He twitches his raincoat off the table. Inside it, of course, is the Buddha, which falls on the floor and smashes beyond repair. There is a terrible silence. Trying to keep his voice under control:*]

Do you know what that statue was worth? Do you? More money than you'll ever see in your whole life, even if you sell every piece of that nasty, rusty rubbish. [*With the quietness of the mad*] I think I'm going to have to smash you, Brindsley.

BRINDSLEY [*nervously*]: Now steady on, Harold ... don't be rash ...

HAROLD: Yes, I'm very much afraid I'll have to smash you ... Smash for smash – that's fair do's. [*He pulls one of the long metal*

prongs out of the sculpture.] Smash for smash. Smash for *smash*!
[*Insanely he advances on* BRINDSLEY *holding the prong like a sword,
the taper burning in his other hand.*]

BRINDSLEY [*retreating*]: Stop it, Harold; You've gone mad.

COLONEL: Well done, sir. I think it's time for the reckoning. [*The*
COLONEL *grabs the other prong and also advances.*]

BRINDSLEY [*retreating from them both*]: Now just a minute, Colonel.
Be reasonable! ... Let's not revert to savages! ... Harold, I
appeal to you – you've always had civilized instincts! Don't join
the Army! ...

CAROL [*grimly advancing also*]: Get him, Daddy! Get him! Get him!

BRINDSLEY [*horrified at her*]: Carol!

CAROL [*malevolently*]: Get him! Get him! Get him! Get ...

BRINDSLEY: *Clea!*

[CLEA *leaps up and blows out the taper. Lights up.*]

COLONEL: Dammit!

[CLEA *grabs* BRINDSLEY'*s hand and pulls him out of danger.*]

[*To* CLEA] Careful, my little Dumpling. Keep out of the way.

HAROLD [*to* CAROL]: Hush up, Colonel. We'll be able to hear
them breathing.

COLONEL: Clever idea! Smart tactics, sir!

[*Silence. They listen.* BRINDSLEY *climbs carefully onto the table and
silently calls* CLEA *up after him.* HAROLD *and the* COLONEL, *prod-
ding and slashing the darkness with their swords, grimly hunt their
quarry. Twenty seconds. Suddenly, with a bang* SCHUPPANZIGH
*opens the trap from below. Both men advance on it warily. The
electrician disappears again below. They have almost reached it, on
tiptoe, when there is another crash – this time from the hall. Someone
has again tripped over the milk bottles.* HAROLD *and the* COLONEL
immediately swing round and start stalking upstage, still on tiptoe.

Enter GEORG BAMBERGER. *He is quite evidently a millionaire.
Dressed in the Gulbenkian manner, he wears a beard, an eyeglass, a
frock-coat, a top hat and an orchid. He carries a large deaf aid.
Bewildered, he advances into the room. Stealthily, the two armed men*

stalk him upstage as he silently gropes his way downstage and passes between them.]

BAMBERGER [*speaking in a middle-aged German voice, as near to the voice of* SCHUPPANZIGH *as possible*]: Hallo, please! Mr Miller? [HAROLD *and the* COLONEL *spin round in a third direction.*]

HAROLD: Oh, it's the electrician!

BAMBERGER: Hallo, please?

COLONEL: What the devil are you doing up here? [SCHUPPANZIGH *appears at the trap.*] Have you mended the fuse?

HAROLD: Or are you going to keep us in the dark all night?

SCHUPPANZIGH: Don't worry. The fuse is mended. [*He comes out of the trap.* BAMBERGER *goes round the stage, right.*]

HAROLD: Thank God for that.

BAMBERGER [*still groping around*]: Hallo, please? Mr Miller – vere are you? Vy zis darkness? Is a joke, yes?

SCHUPPANZIGH [*incensed*]: Ah, no! That is not very funny, good people – just because I am a foreigner, to imitate my voice. You English can be the rudest people on earth!

BAMBERGER [*imperiously*]: Mr Miller! I have come here to give attention to your sculptures!

SCHUPPANZIGH: *Gott in Himmel!*

BAMBERGER: *Gott in Himmel!*

BRINDSLEY: God, it's him! Bamberger!

CLEA: He's come!

HAROLD: Bamberger!

COLONEL: Bamberger! [*They freeze. The millionaire sets off, left, towards the open trap.*]

BRINDSLEY: Don't worry. Mr Bamberger. We've had a fuse, but it's mended now.

BAMBERGER [*irritably*] Mr Miller!

CLEA: You'll have to speak up. He's deaf.

BRINDSLEY [*shouting*]: Don't worry, Mr Bamberger! We've had a fuse, but it's all right now!...

[*Standing on the table, he clasps* CLEA *happily.* BAMBERGER *misses the trap by inches.*]

Oh, Clea, that's true. Everything's all right now! Just in the nick of time!

[*But as he says this* BAMBERGER *turns and falls into the open trapdoor.* SCHUPPANZIGH *slams it to with his foot.*]

SCHUPPANZIGH: So! Here's now an end to your troubles! Like Jehovah in the Sacred Testament, I give you the most miraculous gift of the Creation! Light!

CLEA: Light!

BRINDSLEY: Oh, thank God. *Thank God!*

[SCHUPPANZIGH *goes to the switch,*]

HAROLD [*grimly*]: I wouldn't thank Him too soon, Brindsley, if I were you!

COLONEL: Nor would I, Brindsley, if I were you!

CAROL: Nor would I, Brinnie Winnie, if I were you!

SCHUPPANZIGH [*grandly*]: Then thank *me!* For I shall play God for this second! [*Clapping his hands*] Attend all of you. God said: 'Let there be light!' And there was, good people, suddenly! – astoundingly! – instantaneously – inconceivably – inexhaustibly – inextinguishably and eternally – LIGHT!

[SCHUPPANZIGH, *with a great flourish, flicks the light switch. Instant darkness. The turntable of the gramophone starts up again, and with an exultant crash the Sousa March falls on the audience – and blazes away in the black.*]

END

FOR THE BEST IN PAPERBACKS, LOOK FOR THE 🐧

In every corner of the world, on every subject under the sun, Penguin represents quality and variety – the very best in publishing today.

For complete information about books available from Penguin – including Pelicans, Puffins, Peregrines and Penguin Classics – and how to order them, write to us at the appropriate address below. Please note that for copyright reasons the selection of books varies from country to country.

In the United Kingdom: Please write to *Dept E.P., Penguin Books Ltd, Harmondsworth, Middlesex, UB7 0DA*

If you have any difficulty in obtaining a title, please send your order with the correct money, plus ten per cent for postage and packaging, to *PO Box No 11, West Drayton, Middlesex*

In the United States: Please write to *Dept BA, Penguin, 299 Murray Hill Parkway, East Rutherford, New Jersey 07073*

In Canada: Please write to *Penguin Books Canada Ltd, 2801 John Street, Markham, Ontario L3R 1B4*

In Australia: Please write to the *Marketing Department, Penguin Books Australia Ltd, P.O. Box 257, Ringwood, Victoria 3134*

In New Zealand: Please write to the *Marketing Department, Penguin Books (NZ) Ltd, Private Bag, Takapuna, Auckland 9*

In India: Please write to *Penguin Overseas Ltd, 706 Eros Apartments, 56 Nehru Place, New Delhi, 110019*

In Holland: Please write to *Penguin Books Nederland B.V., Postbus 195, NL–1380AD Weesp, Netherlands*

In Germany: Please write to *Penguin Books Ltd, Friedrichstrasse 10–12, D–6000 Frankfurt Main 1, Federal Republic of Germany*

In Spain: Please write to *Longman Penguin España, Calle San Nicolas 15, E–28013 Madrid, Spain*

In France: Please write to *Penguin Books Ltd, 39 Rue de Montmorency, F-75003, Paris, France*

In Japan: Please write to *Longman Penguin Japan Co Ltd, Yamaguchi Building, 2–12–9 Kanda Jimbocho, Chiyoda-Ku, Tokyo 101, Japan*